T0380336

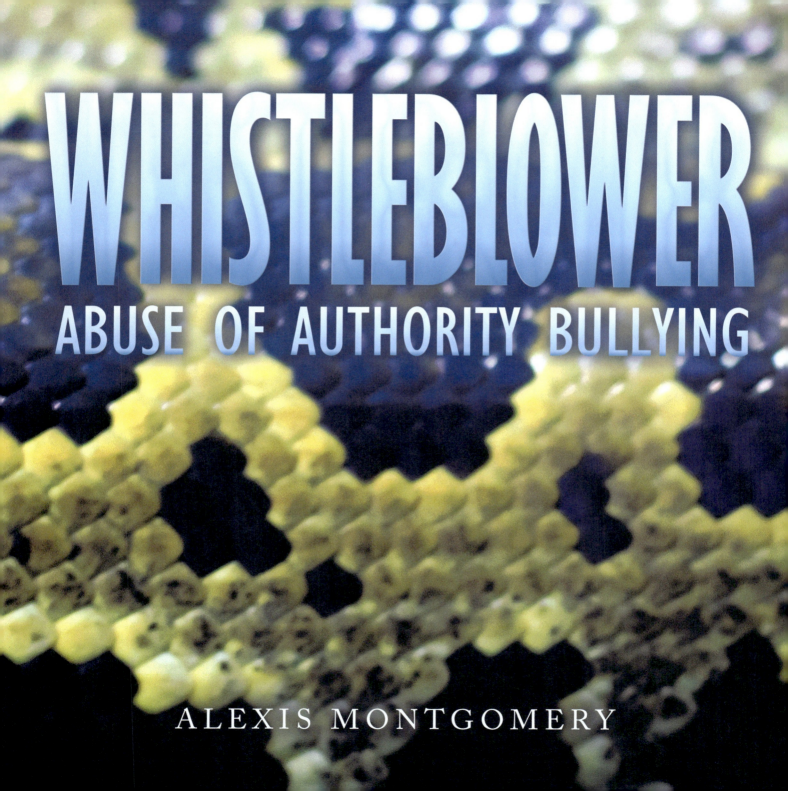

WHISTLEBLOWER

ABUSE OF AUTHORITY BULLYING

ALEXIS MONTGOMERY

AuthorHouse™
1663 Liberty Drive
Bloomington, IN 47403
www.authorhouse.com
Phone: 833-262-8899

ISBN: 978-1-6655-1391-3 (sc)
ISBN: 978-1-6655-1393-7 (hc)
ISBN: 978-1-6655-1392-0 (e)

Print information available on the last page.

Published by AuthorHouse 07/13/2022

authorHOUSE®

CONTENTS

INTRODUCTION

My name is Alexis Montgomery, I am the daughter of Everlena Williams.

My mother made sure we didn't want for nothing. I am the third child of eleven children. I grew up in a neighborhood, where everyone looks after each other's children. She was an amazing woman. My mother made sure we didn't want for anything. When she went to the commissary, she would come out with seven baskets of food. One of the baskets would be filled with cereal and milk. My mother cooked six meals a day. People were always at our house. We lived in a six-bedroom house. She started working for Non-Appropriated Fund (NAF) for many years, and when that job ended, she started housekeeping for rich people. Every summer, she rented rooms to seasonal workers from Florida. She fed a lot of the military troops stationed at the Airbase, Beaufort and the Military Depot, Parris Island. They called her "Sugar Mama

I grew up in a close-net family, where we prayed and partied together. Hellen Burrell was my godmother, she named me Alexis. It took me until I was way into my 30's to appreciate my name. My godmother would take me fishing, crabbing, and we would always have picnics on her lawn at her home. She was an amazing piano player. During the summer, my sisters and I would take a green bus to vacation Bible school for summer camp. The summer camp was held on the beach on Lady's Island Beaufort, S.C. I remember when I was 12 years old, when I accepted Christ as my Savior, on the beach. When I was baptized on the beach, the Pastor and I wore a white sheet during baptism. I was always a quiet person. I used to sit back and observe things and suck my thumb. One day, my mother took me with her to take my grandmother home to Yamasee, S.C. I was about eight years old. My mother entered a construction site, as she drove up the hill. I heard a "voice" and got up from the back seat, and looked through the back window. It was the construction workers who "called out loud to come back". My mother was so busy talking to Grandma and wasn't paying attention. I told her that a man was waving to come back. She turned around, went back, and saw the road was divided, and it was a long drop.

I remember when we used to play house outside, we built a house out of plywood. When we made blueberry pies, we would go across the street and tell our neighbor that our mother wanted to borrow a cup of sugar. She never found out what we were doing. It was four girls, one guy, he always played the role of the husband. We would take turns being his wife. When the husband took the wife out for dinner, he carried her to the edge of the bushes, pushed her in and "ran back to the house". We had the most fun, playing house.

When I graduated from Beaufort High School, I attended Voorhees College in Denmark, S.C., studied Business Administration. I left school in 1981 and moved to Atlanta, GA. Later in life, when I was in my late 40s, I learned that I was dyslexic.

I think I was in the second grade when this happened. I was placed in a special class. I went home, and told my mother that they had placed me in this class without her permission. The next day, she took me to school to talk to the principal, and I was placed back in my regular class. I remember being teased and bullied in elementary and middle school. Rumors were going around that I said I was going to fight this girl. That afternoon, I crossed the street when someone pushed me into the girl and the fight began. The security guard stopped the fight and took us to the principal's office. My mother always said if you get into a fight at school when you come home, "be ready to get a whipping". "The next week, another girl wanted to fight me". After school, I ran home, and there was an army of people behind me. My mother was waiting for me. She stepped out the door and said, "What is going on?" The girl who wanted to fight me, her sister, said I pushed her, I said, she story. The only thing the girl could say was "story in the book here".

I didn't know something was wrong with me, other than I had bad eczema, and they teased me about it. When I got to middle school, it started again. I went to the office during lunch, and asked if they had any work in the office that I could help with. From time to time, that is where I spent my lunch hours. When I was in college, I remember studying for a test, and not remembering what I studied. I attended summer school twice. The last time I went to summer school was my third year at college. My grade point average dropped, and I had to sit out for a semester. I never told my mother. When the fall semester came, I pretended I was going back to school and moved to Atlanta, GA. When I got there, my uncle told me to call my mother to tell her I was here in Atlanta. It took me a while to call my mother, I was afraid. Now, I have a son, and I know what it feels like. When he was in college, I had to contact Billy Needling, in the Registrar Department, to find my son and have him call me. It's called "karma". The weird thing about dyslexia. I always did excellent work. No one gave me any handouts. I was a leader, and I was the go-to person in my career.

My first job in Atlanta, GA was at Burger King, it was down the street from the colleges. Every time the college students came at lunchtime, it was always a line out the door. I would go upfront, and start telling the people in the back, who were making the sandwich, what I wanted on the landing zone unit, right now. After 30 minutes, I turned around and the lobby was cleared. I wasn't even a team leader. Every time it's lunchtime and the line is outside the door, they ask for me. I was asked to be a manager. I began training other Burger King employees. I went from store to store. One day I entered the back door of the store, it was $50 lying on the floor. I picked it up, and shared it with that colleague, who saw it. Then she told the manager, and he fired me. That taught me a lesson, not to share money. The trust was gone, it was time to go "everything is timing". When one door closed, another was waiting and already opened. It was time for me to meet other people.

I still didn't realize that I had dyslexia when I lived in Atlanta.
I only saw that I was getting things done for people, I didn't even recognize that I was gifted. I learn to manage it by taking my time, so I don't make mistakes. Later in life, I noticed I was gifted. I started helping people who wanted to move toward the future. I would have good dreams and bad dreams about people and tell them what I dreamed of them. I would only tell them good dreams, it comes with responsibility.

I became a profiler, and among other things, reading people's body language, exposed them,etc. People would come to me with concerns, "sometimes out of the blue," I would just come out and tell them what will happen or dream of a dream. I walked away and surprised myself, "asking how did I know that?" Everyone on this earth is placed here for a purpose. I know my purpose and have acted on it according to God's will.

CALIBER COMMUNICATION, INC 1984

In May 1984, I started working for Caliber Communication and enjoyed working for Caliber. The people were nice and family-oriented. We went to lunch together, and always had the most fun in the workplace, everyday. My team leader was the coolest person, and has a great personality. Her hair was so long, it reached her ankle. I asked her if she was worried about her hair falling in the toilet. She said, always. One day, she returned from the restroom, saying "owie" as she held her hair in her hand. I asked her what happened, and the rest was history. She treated me like one of her family members, she always looked after me. One day, the director told everyone he was throwing a party at his house. I decided to go to the party. I asked my team leader if she was going? She said, no.

The party was the weekend coming up. During that week, I was pulled to the side and told I could not attend the party, because it was only for white people. I told her then, I will not be going, and thanked her. In October 1985, I said goodbye to Caliber Communications. I received a letter of appreciation and was told that if I ever return, they will rehire me.

MEMORIES I REMEMBER

- I remember my neighbor owning a nightclub. Douglas would always stop by the house on Friday nights, asking my mother to let the girls come out to the club.

- I remember L.F. used to take me and her cousin G.F. to the tennis court on Boundary Street twice a week, and teach us how to play tennis.

- I remember our pastor stopping at our house every Sunday after church to talk to my mother about her girls. He would always leave with a slice of cake or pie. I love my Pastor and his wife. They were always supported.

- I remember L. B. and I were majorettes, and we participated in the Savannah parade.

- I remember when I was a cheerleader in high school, G. F., and I had so much fun.

- I remember I almost drowned at Lady Island beach. The wave pushed me further out. Then something said, "hold your arm out and be still, and it surpassed". It was the spirit of the Lord. Thank you, Lord.

- I remember when I was a cheerleader in college and was called Mikey. After the games, we went to a restaurant, and I ate more than the funds given to the cheerleaders allowed. I had a lot of energy. I remember getting a standing ovation from the audience after a cheerleading performance. On the night of the awards, I took home three trophies.

- I remember when I lived in Oceanside, California. D.W. and I would be riding down Pacific Coast Highway 101, singing Tina Maria song's with the sunroof off. "Ooo La La La, and Naked to the world". We would play it over and over again.

- I remember meeting B. E., a neighbor we partied in San Diego. One night, she asks me to go with her to Los Angeles to catch up with her used-to-be, next-door neighbor from New York. She introduced me to her friend, whom was related to "The Wayne Brothers". She said the grandmother of the Wayans Brothers babysit her sister. We party hard all night. Then she had another party, but I could not make it.

- I remember when my boyfriend came home with tickets to the Los Angeles comedy club. I invited myself as the guest of Damon Wayans, he performed that night, and it was awesome. I sat in the VIP selection. After the show, I walked up to him and introduced myself. I told him to tell Dee I said, "Hello". I am not sure if that was her name."He looked at me strangely", then said, okay. I wouldn't, dear, try that today.

- I remember, when I lived in Hawaii, my girlfriend E. N. and I would go to the Holiday Inn, get up on stage, sing Karaoke, to pass the time away. This would fasten time, while our husbands were away, at war.

- I remember when I worked for an agency in Indianapolis, Indiana, a colleague D. M. and I fellowship, at the Chapel, and on Tuesdays Bible Study. She invited me to her house on holidays, she always had my back. She has a beautiful family, and her boys were funny. We would always take our breaks and walk together. One day, she asked me "how come I never have a dream about her?" I told her because you have money, and I just see you as retiring. After leaving ALAF in August 2013, we didn't get to talk that often. One day, she flew out to Arizona to spend time with her daughter. I took my son to school at the Art Intuition, of Hollywood. How ironic that we both were on Santa Monica Pier simultaneously and did not run into each other.

- I remember partying six days a week in Atlanta. I first stayed in Decatur, GA. My neighbor S.W. from S.C. attended Clark College in Atlanta. We were able to get together and go out partying. My neighbor, S.W., introduces me to her best friend, Cie Cie, and their other friends. One of our favorite clubs of the times was Mr. V's Figure 8 on Campbellton Road. Tuesday nights were lady's nights, and Sunday nights were mini-skirt contest nights. I occasionally participate in the mini-skirt competition. The NBA player, Dominique Wilkins, was a regular at Mr. V. Figure-8. The bar was about 15 meters long. I remember staring across the bar at Dominique as he "worked" the room. He was famous for inviting celebrities, which helped boots Mr. V.'s Figure-8 business. Once I moved to California, Cie Cie would invite me to come along with her, to Warner Brothers and Records. I treated Cie Cie like a celebrity. Cie

Cie was always accommodating in the VIP section. Everyone would hail, too, Cie Cie. She remembers almost every celebrity she has photographed with.

- I remember during the Christmas Holiday, when I was a teenager. People came to our house singing Christmas carols. Once they were finished, I left with them to sing Christmas carols, to other people's houses. My mother asks my sister, where is Alexis? My sister says she left with the people singing Christmas song's. Don't you just love Christmas?

- I remember, when I was a teenager, my sister and I went to Six Flags, Atlanta, Ga. We had the opportunity to ride the rollercoaster, with James Brown and his family. They allowed a limited number of people on the roller coasters. It was amazing to ride with the "Godfather of Soul".

- I remember the last Arsenio Hall show, when James Brown performed. I almost didn't get to see his performance. I was up at 5:00 a.m., waiting in line to get free tickets for the Arsenio Hall show. I stood in line for two hours, then someone came out at 7:00 a.m. and said no more tickets. "I was furious", because I stood out there since 5 a.m. and still didn't get tickets. I saw a young lady my friend introduced me, C. C., who came in to work at Arsenio Hall Show. It was one of his administrators, C. C., I told her they had no more tickets. She told me they will hand out more tickets I needed to wait in line, and they did. Every time the audience stood up and clapped, they sat down, I continued to stand up and clap. The tapping was at 4:00 p.m. I would go home and record the Arsenio Hall show at 11:00 p.m., with me being the only one standing up in the audience. Now I have footage. Crazy right? On one occasion, at the Arsenio Hall Show, they asked if anyone would like to stand up and sing? My brother-in-law and I stood up, and sang Ike & Tina Turner's song. That night was amazing. I was among and met many celebrities on his last show. James Brown was "awesome" as always when he performed. Did I mention I have a little autograph book?

- I remember during the time I worked for Accounting Lorton and Firm (ALAF). My colleague M. and I would always print out a song, stand up facing each other, and sing in front of our colleagues. "We thought we could sing, and the whole team wanted to hear us every morning for a laugh". There were at least 250 people in this department, and our voice traveled. I told her one day they will move one of us. They moved M. to her department, she was waiting for a space to move into.

- I remember growing up with Candy, Kur, and Cas, who lived across the street. Their mother worked for Chamber Commerce, and their father was a military member. "We stayed in trouble". Recently, they returned to visit our family. We sat down, and had some good conversation about who got the most, butt whipping. Something we didn't even know about, "wow", it was breathtaking". We talked about when we left the house, without permission. Our parents would get a phone call from somebody, telling them where we were. When we got home, they would say, where were you? "I don't know why they ask that question, when they already knew". We often wondered "who called our parents". People are still doing this to us today. Good stories, we laugh crazy funny.

- I remember when I met A. G. and D. G., they were engaged to get married soon. They went to Las Vegas and got married. When I found out they got married, I wanted to do something special for them. His brother gave me the keys, and I decorated their apartment, and surprised them. They recently texted me, and said 2022 would mark this year's 35th anniversary. They said "we still have the red satin sheets you put on our bed". Old school right?

- I remember sitting in my car listening to 102.7 KIIS-FM radio, when Ryan Seacrest talked about having dreams. OMG. That is a "great" conversation. We must get together. I am a "big dreamer". I have lived my entire life on dreams. I often get calls asking me to analyze their dreams. We must get together soon. "Hot topic". I've always admired you. "Cool".

- I remember when I used to model in various clubs in Atlanta. I met Mr. Lester when he was a professional photographer. He was a photographer for "big names like Muhammad Ali". Lester's niece was the twins, who appeared on Bill Cosby's show. He taught me modeling skills, he photographed me all over Atlanta. Most settings were in Piedmont Park, Atlanta. Thank you, Mr. Lester.

- I remember feeling "love at first sight". When I attended my sister's college graduation, I met this Q-Dog name S. H. He asked me if I was coming back to attend college? I said, yes. When I came back, he paged me in the freshman dorm. Then he cheated on me, but I was still in love with him. I was asked to stay and be a dorm counselor. Once we broke up, he would come and page a freshman in the dorm. When he paged her, I would go out in the lobby and act as if he paged me."He got a kick out of that". I sat down and talked to him, until she came out, to meet him. I did it every time he paged her. "He loves that stuff". She never said anything. My roommate and I raced to the door every time he paged her. He always had a "big smile" on his face. We got back together, then we broke up again. After thirty-somewhat, years, he said he knew where I was throughout my career, in the government. It was my nephew, they were both in the US Navy. Did I tell you it was love at first sight? Did I tell you the Q's made me, Ms. Mardi Gras? He made me feel the way I wanted to be loved. "It was truly loved at first sight". We were kids who were having fun in college.

WHEN I MOVED TO CALIFORNIA

Sometime in 1983, I moved to California. Over the years, I have started working for Burger King, K-mart, and then other companies. I met my husband when I was driving an ice cream truck on the base in Oceanside, California. Hawaii is where I got married and lived there until we received orders to return to California. In May 1993, I started working as a reservation clerk at the JC's office. This job requires you to set up reservations for military and civilian personnel on order and space available. Chuck Wheeler, the supervisor, called me and asked, "How am I holding up?" and "if I'm ready to start working?" He was an outstanding supervisor and fair. Mr. Wheeler would soon retire. Sergeant Major, James Freeman, replaced him in the military. Problems started when SgtMaj Freeman came on board. Mr. Freeman's day-to-day schedule was coming in at 10:00 a.m., then going to the bank to make a deposit.

From there, he goes to the gym, and then to the club. When he returns, "he is all dressed up and fired up". Like a mac-daddy, he would start talking and acting inappropriately. He would look at me, in a way like he's undressing me, and say "I like the way you look in that skirt". One day, I checked in a customer, and where I stood there is a cabinet below my waist. Mr. Freeman reached down to get something out of the cabinet, without asking me to move. He brushed his hand against my private area, shocking me. "I yelled out loud that I didn't like the way you touched me". Mr. Freeman said, "I won't touch you anymore." "When he smiled, it makes me want to throw up". One of my colleagues, Connie, said, Alexis, I know he touched you because he touched me, and I told him off. Then she said, "Come here, I want to show you something". She told me to look at one of our colleagues, Sharon, and Mr. Freeman, sitting close-up in the back office. After a while, "I had enough", so I went and talked to an Equal Employment Opportunity counselor, but didn't file a complaint. Occasionally, I would check in with the EEO counselor, which went on for a year. At the time, I was the only employee who received letters of appreciation from high-ranking military personnel. On one occasion, a guest wanted to acknowledge me with a letter of appreciation.

I asked the Colonel if it was possible to include my colleagues? He said, sure, no problem. During my time there, my colleagues never received a letter of appreciation from a customer. "It's a team effort, we're in this together". This happened when a Caucasian, MSgt Wilson, asks for a transient room. This would be on a space available, a private room for the master sergeant. We normally have rooms available for the Master Sergeants, but they were filled with people on travel orders and space available on a first-come basis. When he checked out, he was not happy, he complained about me. The JC's office had a standard policy. When you check out VIP rooms or transit rooms, stop by the office, and let me know how your stay was. Master Sergeant Wilson stopped by the JC's office, and told General Coffee, I was rude and unprofessional. General Coffee assistant, Sam, called me and said, Alexis, who did you piss off? I said what? Sam said, yes, it's a Master Sergeant Wilson in here, telling General Coffee how rude you were. I was so afraid that I asked Sam if he can, cause me to lose my job? "He told me to take a deep breath". He said General Coffee got you back, no worries. I said, thanks.

Do you see "how quickly he could have cost me my job if General Coffee had not known my mannerism?" Mr. Freeman continues to give me a hard time and look at me inappropriately. "I would just stare at him". When it was time for my performance appraisals, he wrote that I was rude to the customers and that I was easy to ruffle. "He said I fail at everything". My colleagues, Tina, who worked the night shift, told me that when I returned from maternity leave, I would not have a job. She said, he wants me to replace you. During this time, I am nine months pregnant. I went to the EEO counselor to talk about what my colleagues said. For a year, she has collected information about the relationship between me and Mr. Freeman. I told her it was getting worse, and I would like to file an EEO complaint against him. It was filed and the results were, he had to correct my performance appraisal and secure my job, until I returned from maternity leave. I have applied for jobs on USAJOBs, hoping that when I returned, I would return to a different job. I like what I did, but I couldn't stay there under those conditions.

After I won my EEO case, Mr. Freeman, supervisor, Captain Black, came to me and said, "He has some paper for me to sign". Captain Black said, "I had to comply with these policies when they are put in place, and if I didn't, I could be terminated." I was less than two weeks from maternity leave, when I received a phone call from the Housing Register Department. It was the same building, down the hall. I was nine months pregnant, when I received a job offer. "God stepped in and said enough". Mr. Freeman called me in his office, when he received the phone called for my release. He hit his desk so hard and said, "Tell me the truth, do you have another job?" I said, yes. Then he calmed down, and said, "You have the right to apply for another job". Crazy right? I could not look at him, I felt sorry for him. "It appears he has a mental problem". He couldn't see himself, he had lost his way. He had the same habits when he was in the military, and transitioned that behavior into civilian life. After I left there, many young ladies screamed, running out the door. When the Park-Red Base closed and transferred to San Diego, Mr. Freeman was not offered his position, to transfer with the job. "Go figure that".

OPRAH BIGGEST FAN SINCE 1985 AT THE JOAN RIVER SHOW

Oprah, I have been a fan of yours since 1985, when you won the Color Purple Academy award. The first time I saw you was at the Joan Rivers Show, you were her special guest. Do you remember me and my roommates? It was me and a Spanish, Puerto Rican girl standing outside, waiting for you in the parking lot after the show? We waited almost two hours for you and Mr. Stedman Graham to come out. "That's how much we wanted to see Oprah Winfrey and her new man, Mr. Stedman Graham. "We told everyone, that's how excited we were".The parking lot was empty, everyone had left, and you and Mr. Stedman were the last to leave. The security guard had asked us to leave, but as soon as he turned his back, we moved closer. The usher who seated us at the show came over and said, "The security guard asks you to leave". I asked the usher to stay with us, until Oprah came out, he agreed. Once Oprah and Mr. Stedman came out, we said "Hello Oprah", and then my roommate said "good-looking man Oprah". They both turned around and smiled. The usher who seated us told us when the limousine passed, do not jump on it. I said, why not? "I am just kidding". That was our highlight for the evening, as we traveled back to Oceanside, California. We could not stop talking about "Oprah and her man". Sweet.

I SHARED MY STORY WITH MICHAEL FOR THE FIRST TIME, WHEN I WAS IN THE COMPANY OF OPRAH AND STEDMAN IN 1985

When Michael and I went to Miami FL to see Oprah's **"The life you want weekend Tour in 2014"**.

I bought the tickets, but I had nowhere to stay because most hotels were booked. I wasn't too concerned, because I knew God would make it happen, and he did. We found a hotel about 20 minutes outside, on the ocean view. We enjoyed the spiritual speakers. The show was about to end in 15 minutes, and Michael said, "I will be back". Later, I received a phone call, it read restricted. The security guard told me Michael had entered a restricted area, and he will be waiting for you downstairs outside. When I met Michael, I asked him, why did he go into a restricted area? He was so excited that he saw Elizabeth Gilbert. He said he walked around, as if he were part of the crew. I asked him what he was thinking? I shared that story with Oprah on her Facebook page, when she announced and posted her Oprah Vision 2020 Tour. That is when I told my story. Then Oprah posted Elizabeth Gilbert's video promoting her book and welcomed her back. "The Power Now."

I LIKE THE POST OF YOU AND MR. STEDMAN FIXING A PUZZLE THAT WAS SO DAUNTING. IT TOOK ME BACK TO A MOMENT

When I live in Florida, Michael and I spend a lot of time putting puzzles together. I had an extra desk in my office, so I placed the puzzle on that desk. When the employees or customers came into my office needing assistance, I would tell them to fix the puzzle, while I worked on their problem. They were always excited when fixing the puzzle, it would lift their spirit. Some stay longer than normal. I had to place a sign-up no longer than 15 minutes. "It's a good meditation".

WHEN I ATTEND THE VISION 2020TOUR

The Vision 2020 Tour was so inspiring. I remember when Oprah told her story at the 2020 Vision Tour in Dallas, Texas. "There was no dry eye in the room". She went through some stormy days. Each time I heard Oprah's story, a spirit took over my body, and I cried. God has a special plan for us. God can set you on the path to achieving his goals for your life, until you recognize your worth, and learn to love the person", He created you to be. "We are forced into a direction in which we often find ourselves in". What we do does not define us, is how we rise after we have fallen.

A DREAM I DREAMT OF OPRAH

Oprah, I want you to know that I am not obsessed with you. I have dreamt about a lot of people and guided them spiritually. I have never questioned God's "why me" that He chose me for this assignment, during my time here on earth. I dreamt that Oprah and I were sitting in a trailer, having a casual conversation. I wasn't sure what it was about. Then I dreamed that Oprah was standing in front of the family house, in South Carolina. Many people were there, but could not see them in the dream. "I think it was this book".

DREAM

In 2005, Oprah, I got a glimpse of you in the future when you were older. It wasn't until you turned 61 years old that I reflected on that dream. Oprah, seeing you at that age shows how your beauty has inspired you inside and out. As you continue to devote your life to others, and allowed your heart to shine, inside and out. We don't always have the answers. But I always put it out there, into the spiritual world, and see what happens. The way the spiritual world works. When you dream of a dream, it is released into the spiritual world, and once it's in the spiritual world. It's final, it's going to happen. "That will be the future."

PARK-RED BASE, CALIFORINA

November 1995, I was officially working for the federal government.

I accepted a position as secretary. My daily work consisted of processing letters of request for military retirees to stay in military housing past their ERD. This extension will help them transition into civilian life and make it easier. I work directly for the JS's office, I wasn't a secretary material. I am grateful for being hired into the housing office, considering I was nine months pregnant at the time. But after I returned, things were good at first. Like I said, my job was to write letters of approval, or disapproval, as requested by the retired military. My colleague said, once you get your foot in the door, you can apply for another job. She said that's what she did. There were times when I was unable to get the letters out on time.

The letter goes through three other supervisors to ensure that the letter is intended for what the military member has requested. Director Mr. Roberts called me into his office and said, "The JS's secretary, Ms. White, inquired about a letter that should have gone out a week ago". I told Director, Roberts, that the supervisors keep changing the letter. It looks as if the supervisors were trying to compete. There was a lady, D.R., the previous secretary. When it came to processing letters, she was an expert. She would always be willing to help me when it got overwhelming. When I took the letter to the first supervisor, Sharon, she asked me who wrote this part? Then she made changes to the letter, then the next supervisor would ask and say the same thing. "They know who wrote that part of the letter." This is why the letter was delayed. The letter started going out promptly. Sharon had insomnia, was smart, knew the regulation policies, with her eyes closed, but acted like a Sergeant Major. Some days when she didn't get any sleep, which was all the time, she called us into the office one by one and told us what we were doing wrong. One day, one of the colleagues, who was sitting in the supervisor's office, ran out of the office crying. Now it was my time to go into her office, my colleagues said, to go in with a notepad.

After sitting in their listing, Ms. Sharon said, "She's going to write me up". "I snapped" and told her "I was going to write her up". Once I left her office, I went to lunch and stopped at the Equal Employment Opportunity office. I asked the Equal Employment Opportunity Counsellor to talk to Mrs. Sharon. He asked me, what do you want me to do? I said I want her to stop writing me up, because she is trying to fire me. The EEO counselor came into the office the next day and talked to Mr. Roberts. The director came into the area and went into Ms. Sharon's office. One day, when I was on my way to lunch, I saw the director go into the Human Resources office. "I thought to myself, is he going to fire me?" A week later, there was a job opening in the budget department. I received a phone call, "from a person telling me to apply for that position". The voice on the other end of the phone said, "The job was created for you, it reflects your resume". I applied for the position and started working directly for Director, Mr. Roberts. Soon we were informed that Park-Red Base was on the list of base closures. This became stressful for everybody, I was placed on the priority placement list. I started applying for jobs, every day until "I had a dream".

A DREAM I HAD AT PARK-RED BASE FROM 1995-1998

One night in January, I dreamed that I was moving to San Diego in March, for a job offer. In the dream, I was sitting at my desk checking a military member out of base housing. The military member asks me when the base closes, will you relocate? "I said, in the dream, I am going to San Diego". "He said, when?" "I said, in March". When I woke up, I was so happy. I went to work and shared the dream with all my colleagues. The response from my colleagues was, "why do you think you will get a job before us?" I said because God told me in a dream that I was going to San Diego in March. Once it's released into the spiritual world, it's final. They looked at me, and said, "right", and then I said it was going to happen. March came, and it was getting to the end of the month. My colleagues started teasing me, saying "I thought you were leaving in March". I looked up to the ceiling and said, "Lord, you said March". Just as the month ended in two days, HR personnel called me and said, "I have a job offer for you in San Diego." My dream came true". Before I left for San Diego, I told two of my colleagues that one would leave in April, and the other in May. Not too long after, I received a call from my colleagues asking me how I knew? I said, knew what? The two young ladies, P.C. and D.R., said we received a job offer for April and May, as you said. I said to her, "I didn't do anything", "I just put it out there in the spiritual world to see what happened".

LETTERS OF APPRECIATION IN 1993

General P. Williams
Staff Academy
Six letters from Colonel's
The Air Show's
Formal President Richard Nixon's funeral. April 22, 1994, set up reservations to accommodate incoming military service members.

TRANSFER TO PAC CENTURY AIR WAY (PACCENAIRWAY) CORONADO CALIFORNIA

I accepted a job with PAC Century Air Way (PACCENAIRWAY) in Coronado, California. I worked for the accounting department, one week and the other, for Accounting Lorton and Firm (ALAF) processing payroll, under this funding. I enjoyed working at (PACCENAIRWAY), which is surrounded, by water. I can walk out of the office less than a block and be on the pier, how beautiful. My first supervisor, Melissa, was very kind, she was down to earth. Every day around 10:00 a.m. I would start preparing the rice for lunch. My Filipino, Asian and Japanese friends brought in the various tasty dishes to go with our meal. We would always welcome Melissa to sit and eat with us, she was so cool. Later in the evening, we work with the lights off, "old hospital building". You can only see the glare from the monitor, then we started having fun. One Friday afternoon, we were "loud and having fun", until Captain Davis sent his assistant down the hall to tell us to go home. Wow, that was nice. "If that's all it takes to send us home", repeat next Friday. My second supervisor Ed was a good-hearted, down-to-earth person. His boss, Debbie Jackson, was a piece of work. When Accounting Lorton and Firm (ALAF) was having their annual Corporate Social conference, Ed asked Ms. Jackson, can Alexis attend the Corporate Social Responsibility (CSR) conference? She said, no. Ed said he didn't know why Debbie wouldn't allow me to go, after all, I was the CSR. He said, "You mustn't give it up". I said, must be, he "was so funny and crazy". Ms. Jackson called a meeting and asked the staff to come to her office for the meeting. Ms. Jackson put everyone's names and grades on the board. She wrote my name, but not my grade. These are some of the little things she did to entertain her behavior towards me. "I said, nothing". There was a "position" opening for me to apply. My supervisor Melissa assigned me to that position, to spearhead, and continue to do the work. I applied for the position because I was the most qualified person in my department and was already doing the work. I had a conversation with the Human Resource office (HR). I was told I would get the job because I was the most qualified person. Once the job closed, Ms. Jackson selected someone else in the department. My supervisor, Melissa, was not allowed to make any decision in this selection. I was awarded $500.00 for doing the work, since I didn't get the promotion. The next thing was the process of my security clearance. The paperwork got lost, and that delayed my clearance. "Go figure that". Ms. Jackson knew I filed an Equal Employment Opportunity complaint at the Park-Red Base. This means they had to start the process of my security clearance again. "Go figure that" I was allowed to continue working in the system, until I received my security clearance. I received my clearance, before I transferred to Accounting Lorton and Firm (ALAF). This EEO complaint, which I filed at the Park-Red Base, continues to follow me. Once I left PAC Century Air Way, Ms. Jackson had my security clearance deactivated. Once I got to the next duty station, a background check was initiated. When I filled out form SF-86, it asked you if you ever had secret clearance? I mark, yes, and with PAC Century Air Way. The security officer at Accounting Lorton and Firm (ALAF), told me that PAC Century Air Way said I never had a secret clearance. Secret clearance holds for 10 years.

SUPERNATURAL GUIDANCE CORONADO CALIFORNIA 1998-1999

"I was so tiresome". I called a friend Diana, with whom I worked at Park-Red Base, in the housing office, and asked her to meet me for lunch at the officer's club. My friend is also gifted. She could tell people their future most of the time, and she is accurate. For example, "one of our colleagues was having a house built". The colleagues asked Diana if she thought her house would be ready at the end of the month, as planned? Diana told her the house will not be ready, they will extend it for 30 more days, "and that's exactly what happened". I told Diana, I was ready to leave San Diego. Does she see me leaving? Diana said, she sees me leaving within 30 days or six months from now. I went home and prayed and meditated, and saw myself somewhere in the south, "but could not tell where". The next crazy thing I did was give my landlord a 30-day notice and flew my son home to stay with my sister, until I received a call for a job. While waiting, I lived in Transient Billeting, and my friend's house in Rancho Cucamonga, California. Three weeks later, I got a call for a job offer. I accepted the position at Accounting Lorton and Firm (ALAF) in Charleston, South Carolina. I remember HR asking me, "Are you sure because this is a temporary job?" I said, yes. I remember after I settled down, I realized how I stepped out of faith.

ACCOUNTING LORTON AND FIRM (ALAF) CHARLESTON SOUTH CAROLINA

In November 2000, I arrived at Accounting Lorton and Firm (ALAF). I worked upstairs in the Accounting Department processing vouchers. After being there for two weeks, I realized that processing vouchers was not my thing. I quickly ask someone how I can get hired in payroll. They told me to talk to the Director, Mr. Neil, or the Branch Manager, Mr. Sutton, about applying for payroll. I was introduced to Mr. Neil, and he told me if I had my resume, he can send it to HR. I had my resume behind my back, and said "here you go". Mr. Neil told me there would be some openings soon, and to contact HR personnel. Two weeks later, I went back downstairs and talked to Branch Management, Mr. Sutton, and was told there will be some openings soon. After two weeks, I received an email telling me that I was selected for the payroll position. Working with the Accounts Process Pay System (APPS) was a challenge. It was not an easy system to learn and "figure out how and why a customer didn't get paid". I had already had some experience with payroll at my previous job, at PAC Century Air Way in San Diego. Shortly after working in payroll, I was given a task to process Canadian payroll manually. "I did well". I learned to process security access to (APPS) and had no problems. I was one of the first candidates to be selected as a pilot for telework at home. "I did well". I had an extremely supportive director, Mr. R. Neil, an African-American supervisor, Mrs. P. Faith, and a Deputy Director, Mr. J. Sutton, that was awesome. I had a team leader, Sylvia, who was lazy. All she did was "play cards on the computer". When employees told management what Sylvia was doing, she would retaliate. I was one of those on which she retaliates. When I asked her for help, she told me she would help me tomorrow, and that she was working on some things. "Really", I asked the person who trained me in orientation, Ms. M. Miller.

Ms. Miller was a team leader on another team, but loved helping. Ms. Miller is a very smart and witty person, knowledgeable, and knows (APPS) with her eyes closed. "Everybody would contest that". I told my team leader Sylvia that I had the answer to how to process the refund. Sylvia said, who helped you with the customer refund? I said, Ms. Miller. I told her it was Ms. Miller, and she blew up and told me, "If the customer says it's wrong, it's going to be on you." I told Ms. Miller how mad Sylvia got, and asked her, why she got mad? She said your team leader Sylvia is still mad, because she would never return from her break when she attended the orientation. So, she told her supervisor. Ms. Miller said her supervisor, Ms. Freeman, always had to step up and do her work. I was told "she holds a grudge and never lets it go." I would bring up this long-lasting grudge later, in the book, at Indianapolis. I was told Sylvia was involved in fraud, the government that accepted overtime posted to her timecard, and "claimed she did not know". I know if I had received the exact money in my check, I would know it.

"These same old habits would follow her to her next job". When I first came to payroll, my first supervisor, Ms. Freeman, took me to the swing space and talked to me about my responsibilities in payroll.

Ms. Freeman always threatened to fire me. Ms. Freeman reminded me that she fired three employees when she was a supervisor at Titanic Shipyard. I told one of my colleagues what she said. She said she remembers that, and told me to be careful with her. Ms. Freeman continues to take me to the swing space. One day after returning from the swing space again, "I had enough". I said, "Let me put this baby to rest". I went to her office and said, "Do you know I know this guy who works as an Equal Employment Opportunity counselor?" Then she stopped. It shows that my previous Equal Employment Opportunity complaint has followed me since 1993. "People who support negative people can't be positive". When I attended the gathering in 2019, at Ryan's Grill sub-sandwich in Charleston. Ms. Freeman started talking about her friend Sylvia, "just out of the blue". Sylvia, "so call friend an African American Carmen", joins in the conversation, I just walk away. When I was leaving (ALAF) Indianapolis and moving to Arizona, I was standing in the hallway with Sylvia's son-in-law, "and here comes Carmen". Carmen walked up to me and asked me if I was going to visit her friend, Sylvia, in Arizona? She knew the relationship between us, she chose negative, "literally ugly".

"Michelle Obama said when they go low, you go high". Charleston (ALAF) was one of the most memorable places. I enjoyed working there, and it felt like family.

On Friday around 2:00 p.m., Ms. Freeman would turn on her music and start a line dance, and go around the office "playing the choo choo train". It is supposed to be a Friday break, after working so hard for the week. During the Christmas holiday, we create a board and put families on the board that is less fortunate. Everyone loves to participate, and they go out and beyond. Each person chooses a family and makes that family's wish come true.

My next supervisor, Ms. P. Faith, was super cool. She was always like a mother to us. She always has your back, even when she faces many obstacles. Ms. Faith was a strong woman with a spiritual heart. One day, I came in and wasn't feeling well. She said, "What's wrong?" I said my head is hurting, and she said, your eyes looked puffy. She said, "Here take one of these Alka-Seltzers, it releases the pressure of your headache." Ms. Faith checked on me later, asking me how I felt? She said here, take two more. I always treated my customers, like family. In 2004, there was a storm in Pensacola, FL. They had to evacuate and come to (ALAF), Charleston to process the payroll. I teamed up with them to help them process security for the Big White House, which was part of my responsibility. When the storm was over, (ALAF) Pensacola folks returned to Florida, and I continued to assist the Big White House on a need basis. When we had our all-hand meeting, Director Neil announced that a lady working in the Big White House would like to acknowledge Alexis and appreciate her support in assisting the Big White House. Mr. Neil said she would like to accommodate you and your son on a full tour at the Big White House, and to just let her know, two weeks in advance. I was surprised, elated, and humbled to be recognized. That was very kind of Ms. D. I was also surprised when I was voted Employee of the Month. Awesome, and fantastic. I had a parking space in front of the building for the month. When the announcement came about (ALAF) closure, the next thing they did came to (ALAF), and showed us films, of the five sites, that will remain open. They advise everyone to go with their work. My work was transferred to (ALAF) Cleveland, Ohio. As a single parent, I chose (ALAF) Indianapolis, IN. I did not know at the time that (ALAF), Indianapolis did not have a payroll office. I was asked to come to Cleveland, and I could telework at home. I needed to do what's best for me and my child, as a single parent. I was already teleworking in (ALAF) Charleston, and was tired of teleworking at home. I didn't mind once or twice a week. My team leader Sylvia left earlier and went to (ALAF) Pensacola, then (ALAF) Indianapolis, IN. It was sometime in April 2006, when I received a phone call from Sylvia asking me if I would train twenty-six people off the street, how to process payroll, and answer phone calls on the customer service help desk?

I told Sylvia that I would think about it. "I should have just told her no".

(ALAF) Indianapolis was still my choice. They tell you to choose where you want to go, "even though they want you to go with your work". As we departed, Mr. Neil said, all good things come to an end. 'We've had some good times". But we all remain in touch at our annual get-together in Charleston, South Carolina.

(ALAF) CHARLESTON DREAMS FROM 2000-2006

A DREAM

A year earlier, Accounting Lorton and Company (ALAF) was on the list of closures. I had a dream that the (ALAF) Charleston site would be closing. I told my supervisor and my colleagues. They said I was incorrect, and if any sites were too close, it would be (ALAF) Denver on the list to be close. I said, what about ALAF Pensacola, FL? They said no, because that site is where the Policy Standard Procedures. They said Pensacola would not be on the list.

These were three payroll offices: Denver, Pensacola, and Charleston. Two days before the list came out, I dreamt again that Charleston was on the closure list. I went to work and shared yet another dream, "they said don't believe her". They told others not to listen to me, because I didn't know what I was talking about. The next day, the list came out, and ALAF Pensacola, Denver, and ALAF Charleston were on the list of closing sites. I told them changes are good, you just have to embrace them.

A DREAM

When Colonel Randolph came to (ALAF), Charleston to brief us on what happens next, he shared a joke. One night two weeks later, I dreamt Col Randolph was leaving in the fall. When I arrived at (ALAF) Indiana, I had to find the Colonel. One day, I walked out to the parking lot to go home, "and there he was". I yell out his name, "Col Randolph", and he turns around. Wow, I only met him once. "Crazy me, shouting out his name". He asked me how did the move to Indianapolis go? I said, great. I told him I had a dream, he would be leaving in the fall. I said, are you leaving in the fall? He said, no. When October came, he retired. When he returned in the summer, he said, in the winter he's in Florida, and in the summer, he's in Indianapolis, Indiana. He asked me what I have for him? "I told him nothing, you're good".

A DREAM

One night, I dreamed of getting a call from an assistant principal at this school.

She told me in the dream that my son had stolen a book from the library. I said not my child, he doesn't steal. In the dream, she said yes. I repeated it to the lady, "not to my child". "She said, now he has a record". In the dream, I was so upset that one of my colleagues took me outside.

A DREAM

One night, I had a dream about Oprah. When I had this dream, it was in 2004, I was still in Charleston, S. C. I was given a glimpse of what Oprah would look like later in life. I did not remember the dream until Oprah turned sixty-one. "It was elated to see a picture of Oprah in the future".

4TH-GRADE ROGERS ELEMENTARY SCHOOL

CHARLESTON SOUTH CAROLINA

This was the Spring of 2005, Joseph was in the 4th grade. Joseph and I went to the Books-A-million, the night before and bought several books. Joseph told me tomorrow will be a book fair at the school library. Joseph said my teacher, Ms. Parker, told us to write down our wish list. "I am a big supporter of the book fair". The next day, I took Joseph to school a little early, so I can attend the book fair. I purchased two books, and Joseph did also. I received a call from Principal Jerry's, assistance Ms. Krum. She told me that Joseph and another child had stolen a book from the library and will be suspended. Ms. Krum said when he returned to school, he had to write a letter to the librarian and me. When I picked Joseph up from school, he could not wait to tell me what happened. He repeated this: "I didn't do it." Joseph said his class was in the library, attending the book fair. Kyle, with whom he friends, came over to him in another area, where he was looking for dinosaur books. Kyle told him "he knew how to steal a book". Joseph looked and listened to him as he continued to look for his book, then Kyle left. Joseph witnesses Kyle, taking the book back to the classroom. He put the book into his desk. Joseph told a classmate Kyle had stolen a book from the library. The classmate went over to Kyle's desk, and saw the book. The student told another student, who told the teacher, Ms. Parker. Ms. Parker was so busy in the classroom, with another student. Finally, with all the commotion going on, Ms. Parker went to Kyle's desk. The classmate told Ms. Parker that Kyle stole a book from the library. Ms. Parker pulls the book out of Kyle's desk and asks Kyle, did he take the book from the library? He said, yes. Ms. Parker called the library and asked the librarian if she was missing a book? The librarian said, yes. Ms. Parker asked one of the students to return the book to the library. Joseph and Kyle were instructed to go to the office. When I was told Joseph had been suspended, I called his teacher, Ms. Parker. I asked her, "How did she let this happen?" She said there was nothing she could do. "I get it", it was out of her hands. I can't blame her. "This is called abuse of authority."

The next day, I told Joseph to get ready for school. We arrived at the principal's office early that morning, and asked to speak to Mr. Jerry. Once the bell ranged and all kids were situated in their classroom, then Principal Jerry met with Joseph and I. Ms. Krum was called into the office to meet with us. I told Mr. Jerry that Joseph was accused of stealing a book from the library, and his classmate Kyle was the one who stole the book. Ms. Parker found the book inside Kyle's desk. I want to know why my child is accused of this crime? Joseph held his head down most of the time, afraid of intimidation of the Principal and Ms. Krum. Mr. Jerry asked Ms. Krum to explain what happened? She said the librarian said she saw both of them taking the book, and "Joseph said he was in on it". Those were "Ms. Krum, exact words". Then it was my turn. I may have gotten a little loud, and looked over to Ms. Krum, and started laying into her, when the Principal said okay, wait a minute. Remember, the "librarian" didn't even know that the book was missing. Principal Jerry sent Joseph to class. This is what Principal Jerry said before Joseph left the room. He said the close association brings on simulation, and Joseph should pick a better friend to hang out with. What he should have said, "You are fired for lying".

I look at him and walk out of the room. Ms. Krum, said I will take him to his class. Once she got him to his class, the substitute teacher said to Joseph, "I thought you were suspended". Joseph said Ms. Krum "told the substitute teacher to mark him late". She just couldn't let it go.

When Kyle returned to school after suspension, Joseph said Kyle gave him a little toy ship and a note of apology. Joseph said Ms. Parker saw the toy ship and the note Kyle gave him, and took it from him. She asked Kyle, where did this come from? Kyle said his father made it.

Ms. Parker put it in the trash. Go figure, "we got to rid of the proof, evidence". The two children were best friends.

A week later, I called principal Jerry and told him I needed a letter of apology from Ms. Krum and the librarian, as they wanted one from Joseph. Principal Jerry said, "I gave Joseph a good teacher". I told him that's not enough. I waited for a letter and never received one. I called the school district to assist me with a letter. They told me I have to go before a board, and they will be meeting tonight. I went to the board meeting, and I was given an index card to write down my request. When they called my name and read my card, they said, "I had to talk to the principal at the school". I said, I have already talked to Principal Jerry. They said I need to go to the school district, the school district sent me here. She said, "Who sent you?" I said, the secretary of the school district. She said this is not the place to address this. "I said, I will just go to the media". She said, wait a minute. She took me to the side, and asked me what happened? I told her what happened, and I needed a letter of apology. She took down my information and said, "I will receive a call next week". She was very nice. I received a call from the school district to meet with them. The meeting was with Principal Jerry, Ms. Krum, and the school district. Ms. Krum apologized. I received a letter of apology, and it said Mrs. Krum retired. I wonder how many other "African Americans" she accused, and suspended. She will do it again, it's in her DNA.

5TH-GRADE ROGERS MIDDLE SCHOOL

CHARLESTON SOUTH CAROLINA

The 5th graders were sent to Rogers middle school. Joseph brought home his schedule. He said he didn't care for his science teacher, Mr. Krum. He said to his science teacher, "Mr. Krum is the wife of Ms. Krum". She is the Assistant Principal of Rogers Elementary School, who accused Joseph of being involved with the student who took the book out of the library. I told Joseph that he could not stay in Mr. Rogers' class and needs to be transferred to another, science class. I told him he would not be in your best interest, "he will try to flunk you". Joseph wanted to stay in this science class, because of all his friends. At the time, I had some concerns. Joseph came home, and told me how Mr. Krum started treating him. I asked him again, do you want me to have you moved to another classroom? He said, no. I started recording his grades on a spreadsheet, and saving his graded papers. One day, Joseph came home and said his back was hurting. I asked him if he fell on it? He said, no. He said, Mr. Krum dropped the science pan on my back. What? He said he was sitting on the floor, paired up with two in a group. When Mr. Krum came by, and dropped the pans on his back. Joseph said it hurt so badly, he screamed so loudly all the children looked. Mr. Krum looked at him, picked up the pans, and walked away. He did not apologize, or acknowledge the pans, fell on Joseph's back. Immediately, I called the Principal, Mr. Conway, and asked if he could meet with me? I told Principal, Conway, what Joseph told me about his science teacher, Mr. Krum, and the history of his wife. Mr. Conway said he asked the teachers if there were children with whom they could not work, which would cause a conflict of interest. Mr. Conway said the science teacher, Mr. Krum, did not say anything. Mr. Conway said he will talk to Mr. Krum, and get back to me. The next day, the principal spoke to the science teacher, Mr. Krum, and the child's home teacher. "Mr. Krum said that never happened". The homeroom teacher said, "the kids did not remember it". "How convenient". I went to the police station, and filed a police report. I met with a young police officer, Bruce, who took my statement.

I gave Officer Bruce names, and told him what happened. He told me to meet him back at 4: 30 p.m. at the station. I came back at 4:30 p.m. to "hear what Officer Bruce had to say". He said he went to the elementary school and talked to Principal, Jerry. I asked Officer Bruce, why did he go to the elementary school? He said, to get to the bottom of what happened. He said he knew Principal Jerry and grew up with him. He said, "Principle Jerry, and these are good people". He said there was "no crime committed and walked away". I said, wait a minute, you say, I had to see the crime to report it? He said yes, "You have no proof, and walked away".

LAST DAY OF SCHOOL

I told him I have all his homework, and the test grades Joseph turned in, and took. I also created a spreadsheet and recorded each grade you gave him. I said the grade Joseph should have gotten is a "B". "He stuttered and said let me see. He pulled out the record book, which he recorded all grades, and said let me see. Then he said he would have to recalculate his grades and let me know. He recalculated the grade to be a "C" and had to refile it with the state. I calculated as a "B". If I had not created a spreadsheet, posted his grades, and kept his paperwork as proof of Joseph's grades, he would have failed his science class. This is part of retaliation against Joseph's interaction with his wife, Mrs. Krum, who lied, and the end resulted in her retirement.

MEMORIES I REMEMBER

- I remember the last day of the O. J. Simpson trial. I went with Staff Sergeant White to the condo and O. J. Simpson's house. I remember cars lined up outside his gate. The gate was slightly open, so I decided to go in and look around. I held my hand on the camera and started taking pictures. I took pictures of his Mercedes Benz, garage, and garbage can. What the heck was I thinking, taking a picture of O. J's garbage can. "Crazy right?" Low and behold, "I got caught". The security guard came over to me, and told me, "you are not supposed to be in here". I asked him to take a picture of me, and he said, no. "Crazy right" He escorted me out, he was nice, tall, and handsome. I think the reason why he didn't tackle me to the ground was that I was pregnant, or "maybe he was a stand-up type of guy". OMG, O.J., that house was as big as a football field. I apologize for bringing it up.

- I remember sending Payton Manning two of the books I published. One to autograph, and the other to keep. "I was a big Payton Manning fan". The people who worked at the gas station down the hill always say, "You just missed Payton Manning". OMG, again.

- I remember D.R. always helped me when I was a secretary. Her husband made my son the cutest wooden table with 4-chairs, when he was a toddler. Every time I visited California, I would call or visit D.R. and her husband. During the Christmas holiday, D.R always sent a family portrait made in a Christmas card. "I try to do the same".

- I remember reading about the challenges I faced, and realized many people and celebrities have experienced similar problems. "It is called dyslexic". I read Tom Cruise, Whoopi Goldberg, Steven Spielberg, etc. When I read Steven Spielberg's story, I felt a sense of relief that I am not alone. The world's most famous film director. "These are gifted people". It empowered me, and I told myself that I would be okay. It has helped many people around the world more than you know, like me.

When I told the people that I was dyslexic, "all hell broke loose." I thought they would understand, but they did everything in their power to set me up, and showed no empathy. "I could not believe the magnitude of these people would go to the extreme". They would force me to repeat the name again and again. I walked into this fish place to pick up the "door dash" order. The white woman told the black woman I could not read or spell. "Isn't that what spell check is for?" This black lady with a beautiful soul was defending me and didn't know me. The black woman asked me a few "test questions" in front of the white woman, I played alone. She tried to prove to the white woman that I am, "not what people said about me". One day, I stepped into this restaurant "chicken stop" and the restaurant was full of people. A young man "white" chanted the name on the door-dash order I had. I am standing at the door, and everyone looking at me. It was so bad that he couldn't stop. I got my order and left. I didn't see him anymore when I returned to the "chicken stop". This happened in four different restaurants I went to, and "four blacks just showed out." One incident was when I walked in "I-hop-long" and a black woman chanted, out the name of the order I picked up. Before I could get into the restaurant, she repeated the name, over and over again. The white girl "smart" had to tell her to stop it, she said it already. In a "sub-sell", a black female asks me many times to repeat the name.

There was a room full of people when she asked me to repeat the name, over and over again. The white boy "smart", told her to stop, she already said it. I went to "Burger Bun" to pick up a door dash order. There is this black girl "hater toward me" Close the drive-thru window, want serve me. One day, I was door dashing, and went to "Burger Bun". She was in the back, and kept asking me four times, what's the name? There was a white male standing next to me, who took note of her behavior. She lied, and said, I said something, other than the name, in the app. "McDowell", wow, not all blacks, one day they speak, the next day they look the other way. One day, they serve me some cold coffee. My friends and I go there every day after work for coffee. They know I ask for "hot coffee every time I come there".

I went to "Star-Busting" for coffee, before I turned in for the night. The little white boy refused to take my order. After yelling "hello", he stood in the window, talking to some people, in the car at the drive-thru. I drove up to the window, he closed the window and walked away. Everyone with dyslexic disorder, symptoms, is different. "In a stressful environment, my brain shuts down". One minute I know the "word", the next minute I can't say it. It's even worse when you walk into a room full of people and you know why they're there. Reason "Good or bad" It feels like you're judged. Because "I am gifted". I don't have low self-esteem, God shields me from that. I truly feel sorry for them, they act like they don't know any better. Maybe it's mental.

"Sometimes it was a negative environment and toxic". It was annoying. I met some kind and sweet people, and their kids made me smile.

"I could not believe the magnitude of these people would go to the extreme".

When they "really piss me off", "I would say to myself, that's alright". One day, I will be rich, and you will still be working here.

- I remember being invited to the White House during the former president-elect Bush administration. Mrs. D. thanked me for my support and offered my son and me a White House tour. I was so excited when the Director read it.

- I remember when I was a cheerleader in high school. I was friends with C.R. I remember when her sister was ill, and she helped care for her sister's children. After her sister's passing, she continued to take care of the children. I left for school, and when I returned, I ran into her and she said she married her sister's husband. I thought that was a great thing to do for her sister, by honoring her sister's wishes, keeping the family together. "That was the kind of person she was". You ask C.R. to do something, she doesn't hesitate, she just does it.

- I remember the pleasure of meeting Pastor Joel Osteen. It was surreal when I shook his hand. I remember when he came down the escalator, I and the young lady said with a smile, "he's not as tall as we thought." When I had the opportunity to talk to him, I got caught up in the moment and started rattling about things, and holding up the line. "Did I tell you I was excited?" After the book signing, I got tickets to Pastor Joel's service in Virginia. I remember when you spoke about your father during the service, it was a little emotional. It's Okay, never forget him, because he's the reason you stand. He is the angel, God has sent to watch over you. I know for sure, because he sent me mine, and my mother checks in when needed.

I'm going to tell you a short story. I was talking to a young lady about text messages. She told me about her family member who passed. I told her I will pray for her family. I ask her how is her mother holding up. She said fine. At that moment, I thought of my mother and said, "You don't know how lucky you are to still have your mother". I was working on the computer and started crying so hard. It was like I was reliving these feelings. Then I responded to her text and fell asleep on the computer. I heard a voice saying, "Alexis" I woke up. It was the voice of my mother, she heard my cry. She reminded me that she was still here with me. Pastor Joel, you are an inspiration to me and my son. My son would get up every morning at 6: 30 a.m. to listen to your worship service to start his day positively.

Accounting Lorton and Firm (ALAF) Indianapolis Indiana

Arrived at ALAF Indianapolis, IN June 2006

I transferred from (ALAF) Accounting Lorton and Firm to (ALAF) Indianapolis, Indiana, due to (ALAF) Charleston is on the closures list. My work was transferred to (ALAF) Cleveland, Ohio. In April 2006, the Branch manager, Sylvia, from (ALAF) Indiana, called me on her vacation, from Arizona. She asked me to come to (ALAF) Indianapolis, IN, to train twenty-six employees off the street. "I told her that I would think about it". I arrived and met with Sylvia. The next day, my supervisor, Ms. White, told me that she was no longer my supervisor, and that the branch manager, Sylvia, is your supervisor. The request of Sylvia, to the Director. Have you ever told someone no, I don't want to do it? Then they roll their eyes and threaten you if you don't do it. Everyone in the conference room saw what Sylvia was doing. "I guess I have to get on team Sylvis". I trained employees on how to process payroll and gave them access to all the systems needed to process payroll. (ALAF) Indianapolis did not have a payroll office. I trained employees as follows: How to answer customer service requests on the help desk, Remedy ticket requests, Imaging, building security, and password reset. I provided them with a user id and password for internal and external customers. Sylvia, the branch manager, was my team leader at (ALAF) Charleston S.C. We never had a relationship. "It's in my DNA to help people". Sylvia told me I had about three months to train the employees before the opening of the new payroll office. The Accounts Process Pay System (APPS), services 14.8 million payment transactions. I trained four people on how to build a security profile. I train the other 22 employees on how to respond to customer requests, by remedy, and how to find it in (APPS). This task was not easy, because people learn differently, and I didn't have any help. During this time, it was just me and the employees on the first floor. Sylvia was always on travel, and when she wasn't on travel, she worked from home. Sylvia always had a problem coming into the office in the past. Sylvia would send me an email asking how things are going. I never made mistakes. If I did, you would hear about it, or it would be reflected in my performance appraisal.

I reported directly to the acting director, Mr. Thomas, his office was on the third floor. When I completed the training, the payroll office opened in September 2007. I had a potluck, and one of our customers from Germany attended. It was a great day. I was so proud of my accomplishment. The customer from Germany Bella has been talking to me about a job offer in Germany. When Bella arrived from Germany, she approached me again about the job. I was planning to take her offer, but at the end of the day, one of my supervisor's friends told me that Sylvia told Bella some negative things about you. When Bella returned to Germany, her mood changed. When someone says something negative about you, especially an African-American person, "it doesn't take much convincing for a person to believe it". Bella was no longer interested in the job offer. Sylvia posted the announcement for the supervisor position on the help desk. I thought she would select me as the Help Desk payroll supervisor, since I was already doing the job. She selected an employee from (ALAF) Cleveland for the position, but he never showed up. She thought I had something to do with him not showing up. I knew him well. I think when people hear about what type of person Sylvia is, they make their own decision. She asked me in the meeting if I knew if he was coming? I said, no. She said, "I bet not, find out someone interfered". Crazy right?

Let's just say, the spirit of the Lord allowed me to see what's going on, and what was about to happen. The next person, Sylvia, selected one of her friends, Barbara, from (ALAF) Pensacola, to be the temporary supervisor for the help desk until she selected a supervisor. She told me that I will continue to process security and take requests. I was the only one who knew how to process security requests. One of her friends came to me and told me to get my resume ready, because Sylvia was going to select me for the Financial Analyst position. The next thing that happened, she selected Barbara for the Financial Analyst position. After Barbara left the help desk for that position, she asked me "if I would do her a favor". I said, what? She asked me to be the temporary supervisor, until she found a supervisor for the help desk. "I said, "Let me think about it". I sent her an e-mail saying, yes. "It's in my DNA to help". An SF50 was processed, and I became the temporary supervisor on the customer service help desk. Sylvia said she would help me, but she was never in the office. Now the help desk is fully staffed. While she was home, she placed one of her smoking buddies, Muddy, to watch me. She came from (ALAF) Charleston. Muddy was supposed to assist me, but she started telling me how to run the helpdesk, after I got the helpdesk up and running. "Where was she, when I trained these employees?" Before I became the temporary supervisor, the employees always came to me about an employee, who was fraud the government. I told them during that time, "I was not the supervisor". This employee, Karen, was Sylvia smoking bubby, which came from (ALAF) Pensacola. Karen had no leave, given herself credit hours and overtime, and never at work.

Sylvia was Muddy's supervisor, certified her timecard and allowed her to fraud the government. Sylvia had previous behaviors at an agency before coming to (ALAF) Charleston. Power Ground's Place sounded off the alarm before Sylvia arrived at (ALAF) Charleston. Chief Rooke told (ALAF) Charleston to be aware of her practice, payroll processing, and negative behavior toward African Americans. When I became the supervisor, I reported Muddy to Director Thomas. Management was mad, "let's just say, it irritated them that I brought this to their attention". She was white. There was an African-American colleague who should have received a promotion after a year. Sylvia refuses to give it to her. Why does someone have to file an Equal Employment Opportunity complaint to get what they rightfully earned? Before the month was over, I had had enough, my blood pressure was high, and I lost weight. "I have very little tolerance for bad behavior". One night I was sitting at my desk, and everyone had gone home. This voice said, "look at you, I didn't give you this position". The next day, I resigned and asked Sylvia to change me back to my lower grade. I asked to be placed on the general side of the customer's service help desk, she did. When it came to my performance appraisal, I received a low rating and $200, when all my Predecessors received more than me, even the ones I trained. Sylvia said my performance was poor. I ask Sylvia to see the data, she claims I did not meet my performance. "Wait a minute, didn't I build a payroll office?" (ALAF) still has not paid me, they are known for not paying people when they contribute to the pay system. They owe me a "helluva" lot of money. "As they say, nothing is free". Sylvia said she missed placed, her CAC.

This is the card you need to access your computer. Then they started treating me as I did something, criminal. She had people watching me, checking how long I was away from my desk, completely disrespectful. Every time I went to the doctor, my blood pressure was getting higher. My doctor asks me what's going on, why was my blood pressure so high? I told her my job was stressing me out. My doctor placed me on a higher dose and told me that if I didn't get control of my blood pressure, I would have a stroke. The harassment began when I was constantly watched. I was told I was gone from my desk too long. The situation was getting worse when I worked under Sylvia, which I helped out. The people at (ALAF) Charleston warned me not to go and help her. Sylvia was Branch

Manager, that's a high level position, to not have a GED. Sylvia once told me she was addicted to a drug, and management would soon mention it. My doctor sent a letter to the (ALAF) medical department. The letter stated I had to be removed from the help desk and placed in a less stressful area, if not I would have a stroke. That didn't sit well with Sylvia, which means "she was no longer in control", to demean me. She loves doing that, she is a negative person and has low self-esteem. They placed me on the second floor of the Naval Affairs (NA) team. Sylvia sent her assistant, Ron, upstairs to ask me why I took security information with me. First of all, I'm still processing payroll. The payroll is processed on three floors. She accused me of taking security information to another area in payroll. Ron was never Pacific in what he wanted from me, he left. Sylvia came upstairs and made a scene. She was loud when she asked me what I took with me. She wanted to know if I took security information with me?

My new supervisor, Ms. Miller, allowed her to come to my area and harass me about security information. She intended to embarrass me, and she did. I contacted the head of security at (ALAF) Pensacola and told her what Sylvia accused me of. She sent me the regulation for security to send to Sylvia. I remember thinking, I used to telework full time at (ALAF) Charleston until I came to (ALAF) Indianapolis, and that was my main job. I created a payroll office with a customer service help desk that (ALAF) Indianapolis didn't have. Once she left, I went to the restroom and cried, ran into a colleague from (ALAF) Charleston. I told her what Sylvia did. She told me, don't worry, "everyone knows she's trash anyway". Director, Ms. McFee, and Deputy Director, Mr. Norton at (ALAF) Indianapolis allowed Sylvia to treat me accordingly, without any respect at all. They took advantage of my kindness. This new supervisor, Sue Miller, was her smoking buddy. "The apple doesn't fall too close from the tree". They have issues, and their behavior is beneath me. That's why I didn't respond to them.

My supervisor, Ms. Miller, watched every step I made. The people who work in payroll and outside of payroll knew how I was being treated. Most of the people in the building "gave me the look as if someone died". I worked in a building with about 5,000 people. Many knew of me, rumors swirled around, I didn't know them. Sometimes they would tell me, they heard how Sylvia has been treating me. Many people did not like Sylvia, and the people around her wanted something from her. "Branch manager, you get it". She was the branch manager, and she had the authority to give favoritism, and she did. She was on the selection committee board, which interviewed employees considered for promotions. When she was forced to step down due to the EEO complaint, the followers of these friends went away. Did I tell you Sylvia didn't have her GED? I was told they were looking for it

New Supervisor 2009

As time went on, Ms. Miller was known for her radical behavior. Rumors swirled that she was hanging out at bars and coming in, going off on the employees. One day, she went off on a colleague in the next aisle, and everyone could hear her. Then she got into it with me. I entered my timecard when I noticed one hour, of overtime, posted on my timecard. I sent an email to Ms. Miller letting her know that someone posted one-hour overtime on my timecard. She accused me of posting the one hour on my timecard. I returned the email telling her I didn't do that. I spoke to a friend of mine, who was a surgeon that processes pay errors. He told me that he received a spreadsheet with every employee's data, SSN, hours, overtime, etc. It's a spreadsheet designed to add or correct data information. Mistakes can be made by posting overtime on the wrong SSN, when it should have been posted to the SSN, on the above line. He said in my case it got posted to your SSN, which is wrong, where that person wonders where his/her one-hour overtime was? She came to my desk screaming, "are you saying I am lying?" She continued to tell me that I did this. I did not say anything, remember when I first met Ms. Miller, she allowed my previous supervisor, Sylvia, to accuse me of taking stuff out of the area. I can't say she singled me out because I am an African American, "but the other colleagues she yelled at were also". She places me on a project that a GS-05 salary would do.

I asked her to give me more responsibility, she said, no. I continued to work and was bored, and this was not challenging. "I had enough". I went to Equal Employment Opportunity to inquire about my responsibility. Can your supervisor assign you to work as GS-5 (PD), and refuse to assign your position description (PD) as GS-7 required me to do? The EEO said, don't worry, the auditor will be here soon. Ms. Miller got promoted as a Financial Management Analysis, left but is still in the building.

I was invited to a gathering a few times with good food and wine. This gathering was with a few friends from (ALAF), director Ms. McFee, and about six people. I did not feel comfortable with the subject, Ms. McFee brought up in the conversation. "The conversations were sometimes inappropriate". Ms. McFee would ask her friends when was the last time they saw the previous, Deputy Director, Mr. Norton. Ms. McFee asks me if I knew my previous director, Mr. Neil, from Charleston. I said, yes, she knew I did. "She was fishing for negative information". Mr. Neil is a respectful, likable, fun person, and dear to my heart, he always had my back. When we had a supervisor meeting, Ms. McFee kept bringing up the case when "I whistleblower on one of the employees, who fraud the government". The supervisors in the room kept looking at me. I did not feel comfortable reporting it, but I was placed in a situation as an African American supervisor. I felt this could have been a setup, it had to be done. I just act as if it weren't me and ignored, the others in the room. When I filed an EEO complaint against my supervisor. Ms. McFee stopped speaking to me. One day, she came to my row with her new Deputy Director, Simon, to talk to her best friend who sat across from me. Her friend and I were the only ones in my row, everyone had gone home. "Ms. McFee did not look at me or speak to me." This confirms the agency frowned when you filed an EEO complaint. One day, I went over to talk to the Equal Employment Opportunity counselor, and in that conversation, Ms. McFee's name came up. I told her that Ms. McFee does not speak to me. Soon, after that, Ms. McFee came to my area and walked down my row, and said, "out loud hello Alexis", I echo back. My colleague Gina, who sits in front of me, said what was that about? I said, nothing.

I remember when I first stepped down from bringing a supervisor, then a month later, they indebted me. They took my salary back, which I earned while, I was a supervisor on the customer help desk. I reached out to Ms. McFee by e-mail, she never responded. Leadership starts at the top. "When you take an oath of office, do your job". I was disrespected and humiliated by my supervisors and colleagues, and Ms. McFee knew about it and did nothing as a director. I believed Sylvia would have continued to certify the employee's timecard and would have expected me to. My colleagues were already "hammering on me", waiting to see if I was going to do something about it. How does someone, like Sylvia, continue to fraud the government again, and get's away with it? Muddy was fired, and Sylvia stepped down as branch manager, kept her salary, and decided to retire five years later with a full pension. This is fraud, waste, and abuse, falsifying your time card. Muddy didn't like me anyway. They didn't want to fire her directly, so they gave her a promotion as a supervisor. Then the investigation took place, and asked her to explain? Change roles African American. Are you asking, how long did this go on? Did I say about, a year, people kept talking about her fraud, the government? "But they wanted me buried". Go figure that. This branch manager told me as they left the government. "Come here, don't you ever be afraid to go against the management?"

My new supervisor, Mrs. Heartfelt 2010, kept me on the same task and position description (PD) as a GS-5. Once the auditor arrived, Ms. Heartfelt sent me an email telling me to stop doing that assignment immediately. "I got along with her". If I had a problem, she and I would go behind closed doors and talk about it. When my son was having problems at school, she got information from her mother, who's a school teacher, and shared it with me. Soon she received a promotion and moved on. I stopped applying for payroll jobs when I moved upstairs to the Naval Affairs (NA).

THE NEXT SUPERVISOR

Mr. Michael's 2011 was weird. Management's goal is to focus on me. "You have the right" to file an Equal Employment Opportunity complaint if you have been discriminated against. But "the agency frowns on you when you file an EEO complaint." On one occasion, a branch manager African-American, Cindy, constantly watched me, from around the corner of the cubicle. This happened every day, it was strange. The young lady that sits five-seat behind me, Tina, said she thought the branch management was watching her. I used to run into Cindy in the bathroom, and always uplift her. She was always staring in the mirror, not sure of herself, she was conscious of her weight. One day, I had enough of Cindy watching me. I emailed the director, Mr. King, telling him that Cindy watches me all day. I told Mr. King that this is why people are filing EEO complaints, because of the crazy stuff management does to the employees. Cindy stops watching me. "It's called an intimidation, tactic Cindy used." The team leader made up ridiculous rules about processing, remedy tickets. The rules were, that you can only pull five remedy tickets at a time for processing. The reason why, some people would pull tickets and it sit in their box for several days, or a week. When remedy tickets are not processed, in a timely manner, they are elevated to the supervisor, then to the director. If you pull a remedy ticket, you must process it the same day. The goal is to process the remedy ticket turnaround time frame. Each remedy ticket has a number count, it takes to process that remedy ticket.

I normally would pull between 25-30 remedy tickets a day to process. "As I said, they watch me and don't like me". Ask me, do I care? "De nada". One day, my team leader, Carol, sent me an email telling me I can only pull five remedy tickets at a time. I told Carol when I pulled remedy tickets, I made sure they were processed the same day. She said she didn't care, and these are the rules. I went to my other team leader, Keith, and explained the situation to him. I told him I should not have to only pull five remedy tickets at a time. I told Keith when I process the remedy, it's accurate, and my remedy tickets do not return. He tries to go there with me if I'm one of the people who have remedy ticket problems. I told Keith that I was going to talk to Mr. King about this. "They are always trying to push my button". The next day, Keith had a meeting in the conference room and told me that I can continue to pull as many remedy tickets as needed. He said I was not one of the ones that overextend the amount, I can't process. When we had the opportunity to start teleworking once a week, my supervisor, Mr. Michael, told me that if I came to work at 8:00 a.m., that would be the time when I start teleworking at home. I told him that this is not what Mr. King said, and that is not the teleworker policy. Rodney King said, "Can we all get along?" Michael said Director Mr. King doesn't know what he is talking about. "Just so Bold". Mr. King redirects Michael's supervisor, Cindy, to have another meeting to inform the employees of the correct information about teleworking.

EMAIL THE SES REQUESTING A LETTER APPRECIATION

I sent the SES, James Connor, an email twice in 2021 asking if he would give me a letter of recognition for creating the Payroll Customer Service Help Desk in Indianapolis, Indiana. After no email responses, I decided to contact his assistance. She came back with his response, "no" and good luck

Do you know the cost to build a payroll office? This comes with knowledge, good communication skills, critical thinking, self-motivation, flexibility, determination, and persistence, being a quick learner, good management, and the ability to work well with a group of diversity. The final thing is meeting the deadline to produce and present the product.

I achieved all that and more with the respect of the employees.

I_____ do solemnly swear (or affirm) that I will support and defend the Constitution of the United States against all enemies, foreign and domestic; that I will bear true faith and allegiance to the same; that I take this obligation freely, without any mental reservation or purpose of evasion; and that I will well and faithfully discharge the duties of the office on which I am about to enter: So, help me, God.

Dream ALAF Indianapolis Indiana

A Dream

One night, I dreamed that one of my colleagues had received a promotion and left. I told her and the other colleagues about the dream. If you have a dream, you tell someone, when it comes true, "I can say I told you that." One day, she called me to her desk and said she received a promotion on the customer service help desk, on the 1 floor. I told her that wasn't the promotion I saw in the dream. She accepted the promotion to GS-07 salary on the 1st floor. About six months later, she received the promotion I saw in the dream and left.

A Dream

The next dream I had was for about another colleague. I dreamed that one of my colleagues would also receive a promotion and leave quickly. Oprah also was in the dream. "I still haven't figured out why she was in the dream, maybe Oprah was the gatekeeper". In the dream, Oprah sat in a chair, and the young lady and I sat on the couch. This employee was smart and African-American. I sat back and observed what was going on, and knew she was not going to move up, in the ranks at (ALAF). She received a promotion and left within three weeks.

Spiritual Leadership

One day, a colleague asked me if he could talk to me outside in the hallway. We stepped outside the hallway, and he started telling me about his problems. He has a six-year-old grandchild, who has lived with him and his wife since his birth. His daughter was ill, because of her illness, she couldn't care for her child. He said the father went to court and was given full custody. I put my head down, and thought about it, and said, "You will get her back in six months, if you didn't do anything". A month later, he came to me and told me what he did, which was not a good idea. I told him he should have not interfered. I told him the father will come to you and ask to make a deal, he said why is that? I said he is not capable of taking care of his child. After five months, he got his granddaughter back. I asked him what happened? He said the father couldn't take care of his daughter and wanted to make a deal. Granddaughter back in a loving home.

Spiritual Leadership

I was sitting in the break room outside in the hallway. I saw this young lady, who was in my accounting class, walking up to the elevator. She was smart, and sometimes would be seen spearhead in the classroom, helping the teacher. I remember looking at her and feeling her, a sense of sadness. A few days later, I saw her again, and it felt the same. The next morning, I woke up and began praying and meditating, as I do every morning. I was very emotional, in my mind thought, I felt her sadly. A whisper came to me to give her a message. I didn't know "how and what I was going to say". I went to work and sat at my desk, she crossed my mind again. I said to myself, "Let me go and find her", so I can let go of this spirit in my heart. I found her and stood at her desk, and said,"hello", and then paused. I said, are you spiritual? She answers, yes. I said, God told me that He hears your cry, and continues to pray. Then she got very emotional, and told me she was trying to make a decision. Then she wanted to share it with me. I told her she didn't have to, it's alright. The next day, I sent her an e-mail with an encouraging message. I think it was months later, when I saw her again, she said, she started dating again. I remember feeling that this is not the guy for her, but it's great she was dating again. After I left Accounting Lorton and Firm (ALAF) and transferred to Arizona. I called the payroll office and spoke to her. She was the team leader on the Naval Affairs (NA) team. She said I was dating someone else. She told me what type of guy she was dating now. I remember feeling "she was going to be okay".

All in timing

I was sitting in the break room outside in the hallway. I saw this young lady, who was in my accounting class, walking up to the elevator. She was smart, and sometimes would be seen spearhead in the classroom, helping the teacher. I remember looking at her and feeling, a sense of sadness. A few days later, I saw her again, and it felt the same. The next morning, I woke up and began praying and meditating, as I do every morning. I was very emotional, in my mind though, I felt her sadness. A whisper came to me to give her a message. I didn't know "how and what I was going to say". I went to work and sat at my desk, she crossed my mind again. I said to myself, "Let me go and find her", so I can let go of this spirit in my heart. I found her and stood at her desk, and said, "hello", and then paused. I said, are you spiritual? She answers, yes. I said God told me that He hears your cry, and continues to pray. Then she got very emotional and told me she was trying to make a decision. Then she wanted to share it with me. I told her she didn't have to, it's alright. The next day, I sent her an e-mail with an encouraging message. I think it was months later when I saw her again, she said, she started dating again. I remember feeling that this is not the guy for her, but it was great she was dating again. After I left Accounting Lorton and Firm (ALAF) and transferred to Arizona. I called the payroll office and spoke to her.

She was the team leader on the Naval Affairs (NA) team. She said I was dating someone else. She told me what type of guy she was dating now. I remember feeling "she was going to be okay".

A DREAM

One morning, my son came to me and told me he had a dream. He said, he saw me in an accident, with three other cars, and you hit them. "I said, what?" He said, yes. I have never hit anyone, but someone has always hit me. I called Geico Insurance Company, and told them that I would like to upgrade my coverage. I went to work and told all my colleagues I work with, and didn't work with what my son dreamed about me. A week later, I was at a gas station getting ready to leave, three cars in front of me waiting to exit the parking lot. The first car exited, the other cars followed, the third car almost hit the car in front, and I hit her. We pulled over, she looked at her bumper and said no problem. The next day, I contacted Geico and changed my coverage back.

MEMORIES, OF JEANETTE NELSON

The day she came to the payroll office, we had a connection. She had this kind, sweet spirit. She sat in front of me, and before long, she started telling me what she was going through. She said her boyfriend worked in the building. She said he had been mentally and sometime physically abusing her. I took her to the glass window in the back of the room, where we stood and talked. I told her I knew what it felt like, mentally and physically.

She said, she "suffered from Crohn's, disease". She was in constant pain and unable to eat. I told her I knew what it was like not to eat sometimes. I also had stomach problems. I ate crackers and ginger ale a lot. We share a common interest, not having an appetite, when it comes to eating, but in different ways. "I prayed with her at the window".

As time went on, she told me she had not spoken to her daughter in two years. She said her ex-husband received full custody of her daughter early on. I told her that she had to contact her, and make amends with her. When she came in the next day, she said she tried to call her daughter, but the number didn't work. I told her to call her ex-husband, and ask him for the daughter's phone number. She said her boyfriend didn't want her to call. I asked her, what would he do if he found out you were calling your daughter? She said, he checks her phone. I told her this is your child, who needs to talk to you. I didn't know if he didn't want her to talk to her daughter, or she felt she had failed her daughter, and felt the shame of abandonment. One day, she came in so happy, telling me she spoke to her daughter. One day, she was on a call with her boyfriend, and they were arguing. I told her to tell him that she would talk to him when she gets home.

I was careful about what I said because I didn't want to bring harm to her or my family. I just focused on making her feel normal and praying with her. She told me she had told her boyfriend about my son and me, I didn't know her boyfriend, I just knew he parked in the same parking area that I parked. He never spoke to me when we walked towards the building until she died. I was a bit nervous because I was told her boyfriend knew she had confided in me about him. As I said earlier, I was careful to focus on making her feel normal. A young lady came to my desk, after Jeanette passed, and asked about her. She asks, can I come out to the break room to talk to her? I did. She said, "I worked with Jeanette's boyfriend". She said one day her car stalled out and asked him for help. I believe she said, he gave her a ride home, and then he started stalking her. She had to "place a restraining order against him". She said, eventually they had to move her somewhere else. The security guard said her boyfriend often brought his weapon through security and forced him to return it to his car. What I knew was that rumors were going around that I found a suicide note when collecting her belongings out of her desk. Not true. She always wrote down notes of bible verses. I used to sing "Marvis Sapp's songs to her". Every day before she leaves, she always asks for a hug. I think that was sweet. She was a hugger. I would always tell her to be safe. I would always go across the street to the Mexican restaurant to buy food I could eat and think she could eat.

When she couldn't eat, I offered her a ginger ale that I kept in my top desk. "God loved Jeanette, and I loved her too". It was the Spirit of the Lord that sent her to me before she left this earth. She has been in my department for about three months. Sometimes people need to hear the words "I love you" and a hug. One day, she came in and told me she sent her daughter a box of things, and she should receive it on Friday. When the package got lost, she was upset. I told her to call UPS and track the package. On Friday, she told me that she applied for Family and Medical Leave (FMLA), and it was approved. Hallelujah!! Her plan for that weekend was to go to Atlanta, GA, to meet her boyfriend's family, and hope he would marry her. When she returned from Atlanta, she said she had a great time, but her boyfriend did not. She said after returning home, "they got into it". She said he promised to marry her, but something changed and the engagement was off.

Her daughter finally received the package. She said her boyfriend, and her, have been together on-off for about five years. She said she left him once because the abuse was so bad, she ended up in the hospital. She moved to California to stay with her father for a year. She said he kept calling her, asking her to come back. Her father convinced her to go back, with him, "this is what she said". I'm not sure her father knew the abuse was going on. On Friday, we hugged. I told her to be safe as usual, nothing was different, out of the ordinary. On Monday, my supervisor, Michael, asked me if I heard from Jeanette? I said, why? He said she hadn't called or come in. I said, no, I haven't. The next day, I went to lunch, and when I returned, Michael asked to see me in the conference room. He told me Jeanette had passed away and committed suicide. He said, she shot herself in the stomach. I looked at him, with disbelief, and returned to my desk. About 3:30 p.m., "it finally hit me that she was gone". When I went home, I cried. I kept trying to figure out why, she, would commit suicide. There were no signs. It took me some time to get past her death. One day, I stopped at the traffic light, just above the traffic light. "I saw her smiling face". She knew that I was struggling with her death. That brought me closer. She knew I would tell her story.

CYNTHIA A. WILLIAMS-GOLSON

My name is Cynthia Ann Williams-Golson. I was born in Beaufort, SC on December 16, 1955, the seventh of eleven children born to Evelena G. Williams.

I started my formative years with kindergarten at age 5. I went to a little schoolhouse around the corner from my house. Mrs. Cathy was my kindergarten teacher. She taught me the fundamentals of reading, writing, and arithmetic. From there, I went to Smalls Elementary School for grades 1, 2, and 3. I had incredibly good teachers and remember learning even more from them. Robert Smalls Elementary was named after Smalls, the American politician, publisher, and businessman who was born into slavery in Beaufort, SC. He freed himself, his crew, and their families during the American Civil War by commandeering a Confederate transport ship, CSS Planter, in Charleston harbor on May 13, 1862. He piloted the ship to the Union-controlled enclave in the Beaufort-Port Royal-Hilton Head area, where it became a Union warship. Elementary School was about one-half mile from my house. All the kids in the neighborhood walked to school every day.

Since there was a school just up the street from my house, I began my 4 grade at Elementary School. The Elementary School was considered a White school because there were only white students who attended the school. Well, in 1965, we integrated the Elementary School. The school is still there but is now the University of South Carolina. The names of the African American students who integrated at Beaufort Elementary, besides me, LaFrance Ferguson, Sandra Mitchell, Kerwin Felix, Ronald Daise, Clifford Pringle, and I believe Joe Frazier, the nephew of the famous Joe Frazier, the world boxing champion from Beaufort, SC. We got along well with the white students and I finished out my 5 and 6 grades there. I still remember a lot of them to this day. I have a classroom picture that brings back so many memories of my years at Elementary School. My teacher was Mrs. Sara, who is still living here in the town to my knowledge? I have seen her several times. She doesn't remember me, but I remember her. The years at Elementary School were some of the best years that I remember.

Office of National War Affairs Tucson, Arizona August 2013

I accepted a job from the Department of War Affairs (WF) and moved to Tucson, Arizona. I was glad I knew someone from the Accounting Lorton and Firm (ALAF). My position was as a payroll liaison as customer service responsibility. I didn't have a supervisor at that time, I reported to Chief Devon Rodriguez. I worked with a couple, I was told "they will make your life hell". In the first months, access to the system was granted. As soon as I got it, I started processing payroll. It was a little difficult to work with the couple. They manipulated and undermined your actions. The husband Keith came over to my chair, telling me some daunting stuff about Chief Devon Rodriguez. It was personally and inappropriately. He said to watch how Chief Devon Rodriguez talked to me. He has a girlfriend, and among other stuff he said. I had to take a break, after that he was all up in my face and angry. When I returned, he apologized. They spent a lot of time sending emails and calling the Union and Equal Employment Opportunity office complaining about management. He told me the Equal Employment Opportunity said management told them don't talk to them. He was trying to have Chief Rodriguez removed. When we met with Chief Rodriguez, the Chief would ask Keith's wife Carmen a question. Before she answered the question, she looked at her husband Keith. It's almost as if Carmen got permission before she responded. A customer called and wanted to change their direct deposit. After e-mailing the form to the employee, the wife Carman said you should make her walk here and pick it up. I looked back at her and didn't say anything. I went to the War Affairs (WF) hospital every day to pick up mail and verify funds to transfer to the bank. I stopped by the chapel and prayed about the demonic attack on me at work. Sometimes I would spend fifteen minutes helping a combat veteran, who needs help in the hospital, find their location to their appointment. This was part of the War Affairs (WF) planned, which was implemented to support combat. Chief Rodriguez said he had problems with Keith and his wife Carmen, and to let him know if they get out of hand.

Every morning, I came to work, Chief Rodriguez summoned me to his office. When I went into his office, the first thing Chief Rodriguez asked me was, "what are you wearing?" Then he would look around his desk at me, "from head to toes" and make a comment. At one point, I thought, "He wanted to borrow my skirt." He would also ask me what time I got to work. Which he knew from the couple in the room I work with. I am always a few minutes late. My late timing was passed on to Chief Rodriguez from my previous job. A colleague also called and got the dirt on me, for management. This went on every morning, until I stopped going to his office. This did not stop him from calling me and asking me, "How come I didn't come to his office this morning?" Chief Rodriguez asks me if I have any problems with the couple in the room? I said, no. He said if I came back to his office complaining, he would talk to them. I said, no need. A colleague, Cindy, who didn't work in the room, said, "Girl, come out of that room, you're not like those people." Cindy said I'm the fifth person the agency had hired. Because everybody kept leaving, after working with the couple for a week. When I returned from the hospital and placed the mail in the box, I overheard Chief Rodriguez with his door close talking to Keith, who sits in the room with me. "My name came up". After that day, Keith and Carmen started to retaliate against me. Chief Rodriguez told me that they told him that it took me a long time to process the time cards. One day, Chief Rodriguez told me, "he will sit with me when I printed out, and put the time cards in order". This was crazy, here we go. This process takes up to 2-3 hours without interruption. Keith told Chief Rodriguez it only takes one hour, that's what Chief Rodriguez said. He sat with me for an hour and left. He wanted to humiliate me, and he did. "What an idiot". He calls back from his office 20 minutes later, asking if I'm finished. I said, no. After Chief Rodriguez left, Keith said he told Chief Rodriguez it takes 2- 3 hours to process the timecards. I said to myself, "I know that's not true". I ran across a lady, who used to work in the building, Karen. She said, be careful with the couple. Karen said when she worked with them it was so bad, she was sent to the mediation to resolve the problem, between Keith and Carmen. Chief Rodriguez kept telling me to set up a meeting, and talk to the mediation. I said, no thanks. Chief Rodriguez tried to get me "to do his dirty work to get rid of them". Karen said, nothing was resolved. She said they've been doing this for years, and management can't get rid of them. He sent me to orientation to brief the new employees, and collect their information to input into the system. On the first day, I sucked because I was nervous. After the fourth time, I felt a little comfortable. This was incredibly stressful. Chief Rodriguez kept sending me an email telling me I should go to the meditation. The weird thing about it is, "I never went back to his office complaining about the couple". I spoke to two other colleagues outside the room about it. I told Chief Rodriguez that this is your problem.

They knew I had filed an Equal Employment Opportunity complaint with Accounting Lorton and Company (ALAF). But what they did not know, I won my case, but did not accept the Monetary Award from (ALAF). The stress level was getting worse, I came to work and they played games. I have very little tolerance for their behavior."I wanted out so bad" that I became emotional, and Chief Rodriguez saw that when I spoke to him about work-related issues. It got to a point where I couldn't look at him. I wanted to go off on him, but I decided to wait until I left.

THIS INCIDENT HAPPENED AND IT MADE ME WANT TO LEAVE

This employee came from the War Affairs (WF) in California. He was transferred, so I didn't need to do anything with his records, except verify that his information is still in the system. I printed his profile and placed it in his folder. He checked in and went to his department. When it was time for payday, he didn't get paid. I wasn't in the office when the call came in, that he didn't get paid. The problem was that his checking account was one number off. They said I entered his account number. Remember, I didn't have to do anything because he was transferring from another War Affairs (WF) and his information was already in the system. All I did was print it out and place it in his folder, so I can reflect on it if needed. I was going to send a remedy ticket to Accounting Lorton and Firm (ALAF). (ALAF), can look in the system and tell you who was the last person to touch his record, since the "employee claimed he never changed his record". Once I got back to the office, Karen had already gone into the system and corrected the employee's record. Sending a remedy ticket would show Karen was the last person to touch his record. I wonder if Karen knew (ALAF) could check and see the last person who touched the records. I know these people were lying and working together to make me fall. As soon as the employee entered War Affairs (WF), he was gone within two weeks. They said he was let go. "What a lavish scam". Do you know "how hard it was to take responsibility" when you know you didn't touch his records? The Chief wanted me to say, "I did it". When I said, "I did it, the Chief smiled and said okay". "What a lavish scam, they got me". I don't make mistakes like that, especially when it comes to people's pay. "This was yet another set-up".

My last days before leaving

Before I left, Chief Rodriguez sent me an email telling me that I said something inappropriate to him. I could not think of anything I could have said inappropriately, except that he was inappropriate to me. I reply to Chief Rodriguez's email saying, "if I said anything inappropriate to you, I apologize". I tried to forward the email or print it out, but I noticed he had it protected, I could only reply. I knew he was out of the line. I remember Keith telling me earlier in the room, watch out for Chief Rodriguez. On my last day, I went to the cafeteria. I told the young lady in the cafeteria, today is my last day. She said, "she wondered how long I would last". She said everyone knows about the couple in the office, and they can't keep anyone.

The Chief response to my interview Reference

I called Chief Rodriguez in March 2016, and told him that my supervisor, Hannah, gave me a bad reference, when I tried to leave. I asked the Chief what kind of references he gave me when an agency called for a reference for me. Chief Rodriguez said when they called, he told them, and I quote. **"I don't have anything good to say" and "I don't have anything bad to say".** I said that's what you're telling them. We end the call. He is still mad because I left.

Tucson Arizona Uplifting Word

Uplifting Word

I have always called on a dear friend, A.J.M., in Summerville, S.C., when I get too stressed out. She always has a good word to lift me up. She told me don't worry about it, God will "show up and show out". God showed up shortly afterwards, I left.

Spiritual Guidance

A colleague from the same agency I worked at in Indianapolis, Indiana, said to me. Alexis, I know you are religious, but you better start applying for jobs to get out of here. Jeff said, "You saw what I went through when I sat in that room with them for eight months." I told Jeff, I didn't have to apply for a job, because I've already prayed about it. I told him I had 100% faith. He said, okay. That following Monday, I signed off on my 90 days performance rating, and on Thursday, I received an email from a supervisor in Florida, saying hello Alexis, do remember me? She asked me if I wanted to come and work for her? She asked, if my son was still in Orlando? She said, "Send me your resume". I did not remember her, because when I sat on the team for the War Affairs (WF), Indianapolis, Indiana. I helped all the War Affairs (WF), Human Resources specialists throughout the states. God has answered my prayer. "He showed up and showed up."

FAMILY MEMOIRS

SANDRA WILLIAMS GRIER

Sandra Grier was the owner of the Beaufort Fabric Shop on Boundary Street in Beaufort, S.C. She made about $1000 a day. She ran the fabric shop for nine years until she lost her business after a new Walmart opened up. Walmart sold the most affordable fabric that customers could not turn down. She had another Business making Tailor-made men's and women's clothing.

ANDERSON WILLIAMS

Anderson Williams was a retired U.S. Army and worked as a Civilian Service for seventeen years at the Marine Corps Air Station Beaufort, S.C., before his passing. Anderson had a trade, he loves fixing and building cars. Sometimes we all had the luxury of getting our cars fixed at less or no express. He was the most popular DJ and had the pleasure of entertaining people. He had a spiritual love for people and was a child of God. His blessing has been a memory to our family and others.

JAMES WILLIAMS

James Williams is a retired U.S. Air Force. He was planning to move to another state, but my mother fell ill. He decided to stay, and take care of our mother. My mother instilled in her son's, "take care of your family". When my brother Anthony was born, he had seizures, he outgrown it, but never the same. James was left to take care of my sister, Willamae, and her son, Eric, because they are challenged. When my older sister Dolores battled with cancer for 20 years. James made sure she got her medication, and made it to her appointments, even though she was living in another state. Delores wasn't only his sister, she was his best friend. He has always spoken to public school to the children. James has always helped people in the community if needed. James has always been the "go-to person" in the family. A family member said she needs a co-signer to buy a house. He said, "Where can I sign?" A family member said I need a co-sign on a loan. He said, "Where can I sign?" A family member said I don't have money to come home. He said, "How much do you need?" All my life, my brother had provided for me, since I was a little girl. James, if you are reading this, I love you. "You have kept this family together mentally, physically and financially." For that, I salute you.

LA-TREVETTE FELDER

Latrevette Felder worked at Marine Corps Recruit Depot, Parris Island, SC. She regularly prepared Thanksgiving, and Christmas dinners, for all ranks of military service. She would sew their patches back on their military uniforms when needed. She took care of their children when they needed a date, night or weekend break. When Latrevette transferred to Camp Lejeune, NC, she started baking cakes for military retirement, birthdays, promotions, and other occasions.

LINDA TAYLOR

Linda Taylor worked as housekeeping for the Olsen family in Port Royal Beaufort, S.C. A friend of the Olsen's asked Mr. and Mrs. Olsen to ask my mother if she knew anyone she could refer for housekeeping for the Blythe Danner family.

This is how my sister, Linda, became acquainted and worked for the Danner's family. I remember my sister Linda telling me she was a housekeeper for Blythe Danner (Lillian Meechum) while filming The Great Santini. Linda said it was a pleasure to have met Gwyneth and Jake Paltrow, when they were seven and four years old at that time. She said Mrs. Danner introduced her to Robert Duvall (Bull Meechum) on Halloween night. She said she took her two kids out for trick-or-treating and ran into Mrs. Danner. Linda said when Mrs. Danner would come and go during her filming, she always enjoyed talking to her. She said, Mrs. Danner, has a peaceful soul.

The Great Santini was filmed on 1 Laurens Street, in Beaufort, S.C. This location was three blocks behind our family home on Glover Street in Beaufort, S.C. The houses are known as both Tidalholm and the Edgar Fripp Home, after the rice planter who had it built. Many military scenes were shot at the Beaufort, Marine Corps Air Station. He later wrote; The Water Is Wide based on his experiences as a teacher. The book from the National Education Association and an Anisfield-Wolf Book In 1976, published his novel, The Great Santini. His memoir is Conroy's first book since My Reading Life, a collection of essays published in 2010. Kirkus Reviews calls The Death of the Moving of an unforgivable father and his unlikely redemption." It's one of 10 titles on the latest Library Reads, a national staff picks list. On Oct 23, 2013, Pat Conroy died on March 4, 2016, in Beaufort, South Carolina, at the age of 70 years old. May his memories be a blessing to others who knew him.

Long John Corporation Naval Affairs Gainesville Florida January 2014

When I arrived in Gainesville, FL, my supervisor, Hannah Brown, asked if I could come to her office and meet her on Sunday, and I did. On my first day in Human Resources, I was assigned to an unclean desk, "it was a train wreck". The files were left everywhere. I was told I had to move those files to another cabinet and shred the files that were not needed. The supervisor, Hannah, gave me guideline instructions for what files would be saved and shredded. The young lady, Cookie, who left her desk a mess, moves over to the next trailer. I asked the supervisor, Hannah, why she couldn't come back and clean her desk? Hannah just looked at me and walked away. At that moment, "I knew what I was dealing with, user". When I worked at Accounting Lorton and Firm (ALAF), in Indiana, on the War Affairs (WF), this same supervisor, Hannah, used to call me all the time for assistance. I didn't remember her name, but her habits. She would start complaining about her supervisor, Wanda Fuller. She said, her supervisor, thinks she doesn't work. "Go figure that" I receive a phone call at my desk asking to speak to Hannah. I did not know who was on the other end of the phone at the time. She asked me, did I see all the drama going on in the office? I told her that I don't get caught up in that stuff, "I mine my own business". I started learning how to process TSP, health, and life insurance benefits as a Human Resources assistant. I process newly hired employees and counsel customers that separation, retiring, and resigning are transferred from within the government. I had to train myself, and I was told "it was always that way". After six months, I was ready to move on. I started applying for jobs. When I receive a phone call or email for an interview, I take annual leave for the interview. I had an interview with another Naval Affairs (NA) Corporation. I told Hannah, because I knew they shared information, and would tell her. Also, if I'm gone longer than expected for the interview. When I returned from the interview, Hannah came to my desk and said, "I thought you were going to stay". She said, if you stay, I will train you. I told my colleague Judy what Hannah said. She said, the only reason why she told you that is so you can stay.

LATE FOR WORK

Sometimes, I had a habit of being five minutes late at this job. I can use the excuse that parking is hard to find. Hannah Brown had a policy that when you are late, you can make it up at the end of your shift. Hannah had people watching me, even her supervisor, Wanda. She asked me to watch Tina, an African-American, colleague when she came to work? I said, no. "I did not want to be involved". This is how Hannah operates. She would tell one of her boys to tell Tina, Hannah told Alexis, to watch you. "Hannah loves drama". She also hired an employee, Ken, from Accounting Lorton and Firm (ALAF), about the same time she hired me. I didn't know him. When I went around the (ALAF) payroll office saying goodbye, Ken asked me where I was going? This was the first time I talked to him. I know Hannah was told shortly after I arrived that I had filed an Equal Employment Opportunity complaint against my superior at (ALAF). Within that month, her personality started to change toward me. What they didn't know, I won my case but did not accept the monetary award. I thought by not accepting the monetary award, they would stop retaliating against me. But that didn't stop them.

Hate is "horrific"

DEALING WITH A PERSON THAT APPEARS TO HAVE A MENTAL ILLNESS I HAVE EMPATHY

Hannah talked openly about this, that she takes three pills, one of them to stay focused. She didn't say what the other two were. I experienced first-hand what she meant" when she said she had problems focusing". I was in Hannah's office to inquire about a pay, problem. She began to look over it, when someone else came in. She put my paper down and started to help the other person. A third person then entered the room with a problem. "I said wait a minute what just happened", I was here first. Hannah said, "I know." I said I will return later. Hannah tells everyone she doesn't want to be a supervisor, but wants to keep her salary. She has been "sounding the alarm since I arrived". Since I arrived, Hannah has done 30% of the work and that's given her little exact percentage. I thought she was kidding. She is a procrastinator and refuses to get things done, and she thinks it's funny. Hannah gets mad when customers reported her to Chief Hack. When Chief Hack told her about the unsatisfied customer, that she'd been promising to fix his pay, "she started making up excuses". She also said she would step down if she could keep her salary. "Go figure that". He ignored her by smiling, as we exited. I have seen Hannah in a rage, crying and stomping her feet back and forth. Another colleague asked me what was wrong with her? He saw "her crying at the printer, in the back, doing the same." Sometimes I have empathy for people like her, "but she's a flat outlier". A doctor reported her because she had promised, to correct his salary for six months. "She hopes he gets a debt". I said, "Hey, that's not nice". She said, "I know you're right". Another customer needed his records corrected to receive his retirement. He has been waiting about eight months for his retirement annuity payments. She refuses to correct his records, so the Office Personnel Management (OPM) could process his retirement annuities.

Hannah's supervisor, Wanda, asked me to correct another customer's record and send in a remedy ticket? I told her I did, but Hannah keeps messing his records up. I sent Hannah a message, telling her please don't touch the customer records. She did, it again. Hannah claims the reason why she can't get anything done is she gets interrupted. When she said that, they sent her to an off-site location, and she still didn't get anything done, so they brought her back on site. Hannah just wants to work when she decides, and nothing is getting done.

There is something wrong with this picture. If you and I did this, "we would have been fired". The agency "continues to entertain her bad behavior".

FRAUD WASTE AND ABUSE

Some employees, such as Sam, Lowell, and Stan, would call in sick and not be charged for sick or annual leave. Sometimes they leave for three hours, and it's never accountability for their actions. Most of the time, the supervisor Hannah doesn't know where they have gone. On one occasion, when this employee, Sam, did not call or come in when Hannah asked me, it was around 3:30 p.m. I told her he never came to work, and she said", I thought I saw him". On another occasion, he was supposed to head up the orientation, "but he was a no show". Dan, who was there to talk about the worker's comp policy, spoke about Sam's pay and leave policy, at the orientation in his absence.

Dan asked Sam's supervisor, Hannah, where was Sam? He was supposed to be at orientation, at 11:30 a.m., and he did not show up. She called him and he said he was moving, and he will come in afterwards. What kind of job allows you to come and go, when you want? I was gone from my desk for 15 minutes to the next trailer, went over some information with the specialists. Hannah was looking for me, because the phone calls were being transferred to my desk, and I wasn't at my desk. I was treated as the only colleague, who worked harder than anyone else, as a Human Resources assistant. Everybody in HR talks about the employees missing from their desks for hours, at the highest level in headquarters, and they look the other way because they are not African American. These employees, Sam, Lowell, and Stan, would request overtime and sit in a group talking until 8:00-9:00 p.m. on overtime, and then go home. They would work their overtime during the day shift, and turn it in when they start their overtime, after the shift.

One of the colleagues was caught falsifying his timecard and adding overtime when he wasn't at work. Someone told Hannah. Hannah asked Jared, why did he do it? Jared said he had fallen behind in his bills. Then I was told, Jared did it again. They asked me what time I left, because Jared said he was still at work while I was there. I said he left shortly, after everyone left at 4:30 p.m. I heard he received a promotion after I left. Fraud, Waste and Abuse. My colleague Judy, and I moved to the other trailer to support the specialists. Before Judy and I relocated to the other trailer, her scheduled shift ended at 4:00 p.m. After moving over to the trailer, she started leaving at 3:30 p.m. This went on for at least six months. One of the supervisors asked Judy, "What is her schedule?" She didn't answer the question. Hannah is aware that Judy is leaving early, and "says nothing".

Hannah had one of her colleagues, Ann, who allowed her to sit at the customer service help desk and used foul language in front of the customers. She would sit at the help desk. She was hired to process benefits, but was lazy. While Hannah was away on vacation, "she got cocky". She started cursing out the employees in the workplace. She asked me to step outside, and I did, to see what she wanted. When I stepped outside the trailer, she tried to lower me toward this building. She kept saying come on, I said no. Then she said, "go to hell". I told her, I would pray for her. I often wonder, what would she have done. "She was always fixated on me".It's like she was sent there "in and then out". After Ann had been gone for three weeks, she called and spoke with Hannah. She told Hannah that she had a debt, because her leave was paid out. Ann had a break in service, and had not yet started working at the IRS. Hannah corrected her leave by falsifying an SF 50 correction, and made it look like Ann just left. Hannah wanted me to send in a remedy ticket, asking (ALAF) to correct her leave. I told Hannah she can't do that. I often told my colleagues Judy, when I leave, if Hannah tries to stop me, "I'm going to tell everybody". Another African American, Tina, tries to leave. She accepted a position in the other trailer, still with Human Resources. Hannah wouldn't let her leave. Hannah's reason was she didn't have enough people in her department. She went to Chief Hack on Hannah, and she left.

Interview reference

I had many interviews for a payroll position. One was the Long John Corporation (LJC), in San Diego. They both asked me if they could contact my supervisor? I said, yes. My colleague Judy said Hannah is the type "who decides whether you go or stay." Judy also said Hannah likes boys, and she will protect them. She was not the only colleague that said that, this way they come and go as they please. Hannah lets the boys get away with everything, and makes the women work. I have always felt in my heart that Hannah was given me a bad reference, but could never prove it. I ask one of my colleagues, Lowell, if he thinks Hannah would give him a good reference? Lowell said, yes. I thought about the two young ladies visiting, from the HR private sector, who came to visit. I introduce Sam and Lowell to the two young ladies, from HR. They asked the ladies if they were hiring, and they referred them to their website. I took them to meet Hannah, and she asked them what they did? They said, we are HR and work in the private sector. Hannah asked the ladies whether they were hiring, because she was looking for a job. They told Hannah that the two young men asked us the same thing. "Hannah said don't hire them". Then she said, "I hired two idiots".

All calls and customers walk-in were transferred to me 85% of the time

Hannah Brown told the front desk employees to send all the calls to me and the customers. I felt Hannah was telling the front desk, to do this. I went to the front desk, and asked Billy why all calls and customers transfer to me. Billy said, Hannah, told him to send you all the calls and customers. I asked Hannah if I could see her for a moment, at the back of the trailer? She said yes. I asked her if she told Billy to send all calls and customers to me? Hannah said yes. I ask her why? Hannah said, because you know how to communicate with the customers, answer their questions better than any of the others. "But that doesn't make it right". There are seven colleagues that's a Human Resources assistance for benefits. I am being overworked. "You see what I'm dealing with".

1-ACCUSED

There was an incident involving my "USERID and password" in the system. I was accused of giving my colleague Mark a promotion from a GS-04 to a GS-11. This was crazy. To process a promotion, you need information from three systems. The first step is to look up the employee's name to get their SSN. Next, you go into another system to get the EIN ID under the employee's name. The final step is to log in to the Finance Process Data Manual System (FPDMS), to create an SF50 to complete the process. Once you complete the process of the employee in the system, you have to give it to the supervisor, Hannah, to release.

"I must look pretty darn stupid to them".

First of all, if I gave anyone a promotion, I would give it to myself. "Not the white boy, I just meant". I had already taken a downgrade coming into the (JLC)-Naval Affairs. Hannah said I may have done it by error. I said, no, I'm not that stupid. I had gotten relaxed by leaving my CAC on my computer. I walked away from my desk for a minute to ask a question, and remembered I left my CAC and ran back to get it. On many occasions, I allowed Hannah to sit at my computer when I needed her assistance. She told me to "let her drive and send me to get things from her office". The colleague Mark, I was accused of giving him a promotion desk, sat across from me in the cubicle. I have asked him for assistance, but I never left my desk while he was sitting there. I worked for Accounting Lorton and Firm (ALAF). If you leave your CAC on your computer, someone would take it and give it to your supervisor. That supervisor would make you drop it like it's "HOT" before giving it back to you. "We pulled one on her too". She was cool. Hannah didn't believe me, she insisted I did that. This colleague was no longer working in our office when this happened, but still part of HR. The next day, I brought it up again, asking Hannah why she didn't believe me. Hannah said I never accused you, I said, "You did accuse me". Hannah is a liar, and everyone says this about her. Hannah said she would talk to the head of security, Mark works for. I checked back with her, asking if she called? She said, no. I shared it with my colleague, Judy, and she said, if he comes into the office, she will point him out. I emailed the head of security, Tom, and left a message on his voice mail. "He never returned my email or phone call." One day, Tom came to the office, but did not stop and talk to me. We had an HR meeting, and everyone attended, including the head of security, Tom and Mark. It was held in the conference room. Tom and Mark sat against the wall, to my right, and never looked at me. During the HR meeting, Chief Hack bought up the incident and gave an example "of what might have happened". Chief Hack said the person may have gone to the employee's computer, or given him her USERID and password. "Then he throws some papers on the table to make a point".

This was unprofessional and humiliating, what Chief Hack demonstrated to my colleagues, without talking to me. Tom is responsible for the background check. During the investigation, he found that I filed an Equal Employment Opportunity complaint with (ALAF) and shared it with the agency. "It is called a need to know". In my second week, they showed some animosity against me. My colleagues started hating on me, even some African Americans. "Through Christ, my Lord and Savior, I have faith".

Hannah and I were working on a project in which she owed 290 employees. Hannah attended a meeting and claims they told her to promote all Medical Support. She got a team of males to help her process their promotion. After she had completed the process, another meeting was held where she was told they did not tell her to promote medical support. The HERM guideline that tells you who should be promoted was not published and signed to support which employee will be promoted. Hannah came back to the office and said she talked to Chief Hack, and he told her to ask me to help her correct the employee's salary and process the waivers. That's what she does when she wants certain employees to get credit, but when it backfires on her, now she needs my help. I helped correct the employee records and had to put together all packages for the employees to request a waiver of 290 employees. She still asked the boys to help her correct the records behind my back, "and they made it worse". When I point it out, Hannah always says she doesn't know why they're doing that.

2-ACCRUED

When we corrected the employee's pay, Hannah went to a meeting and was asked by Chief Hack about the update on the employee's pay. She said Alexis had the folder, and she was not able to finish. A few people who came back from the meeting told me Hannah had lied to the Chief on you. "She said Alexis had the folder, which is why she can't complete the task". I went to Hannah's office and asked her which folder she told Chief Hack I had? She asked me if I had the folder? I told her, no. She told me to check the old desk I used, before moving to the trailer. "I knew I didn't have the folder".

I read the names of the folders I had in my hand. I walk over to the desk, and back, just to satisfy her. I sat the folders in my hand, on the chair, and went to the bathroom. When I returned, there was a folder on the floor, under my chair. I ask her why this folder is on the floor? Hannah said she did not know, and said "I brought this folder in here". It was the folder, "she told the Chief I had". On the floor under my chair. I just looked at her and said "come on, let's go over these people's pay". "Her office is full of things, and Hannah would look you in the eye and don't blink and lie". I went over a few things with her, and left. She made me "want to throw up in her lap".

MY SUPERVISOR HANNAH BROWN ALLOWING ANOTHER EMPLOYEE TO DISRESPECT ME IN THE WORKPLACE

My colleague, Barbara, was upset because her signature was on a benefit form, she processed incorrectly. The customer called and complained about Barbara to her supervisor, Hannah. I always say to Hannah, "Why can't my coworkers correct their work?" One of the employees, Tina, a troublemaker, walked back to Barbara's office and told her Hannah, told Alexis, to process a form with her signature on it. Barbara came to my desk, raising her voice boldly, asking for her benefits form. Then she threw the benefits form, in my face, and left. I told her Hannah, told me to process her benefit form. I was violent and humiliated in front of my peers. "It was scary". Barbara walked down the hallway to Hannah's office, ranting and raving, and went back to her office. "Talking about ghetto" Hannah did nothing, just sat in her office, and listened until I went down there. I was so upset, and the anger was so loud in my mind. I wanted to punch her in the face and say, "Shut up". I got up, and told Hannah why did she allow Barbara to treat me that way? I told Hannah, "This is a hostile environment, and I'm going home". She followed me outside and said she was going to Chief Hack about this and asked me if I needed someone to take me home? I said, no. Hannah likes drama. I know she was laughing, "her butt off, behind my back".

The next day, Hannah said, since you said this is a hostile environment in the workplace, you will have to write a letter about what happened. The next day, I came in and went to Hannah's office, and gave her the letter she told me to write. Hannah went into a "full range of tantrums". Hannah places her head down on the desk, shaking her head upset, saying I gave you a good performance appraisal, didn't I? She kept repeating it, shaking her head upset, saying didn't I? Then she said, "She has too many problems". I was looking at her, thinking in my mind what the "hell." She said she talked to Chief Hack, and he told her to handle it. I knew that was a lie, I don't think she talked to him. I walked out of her office and went to my desk. When she came to my desk to talk, I turned around and continued working. This is what she does. This is why "I wanted to get the "hell out of there?" I move on because she doesn't like to deal with confrontation. She said it in one of our meetings. Crazy right? "Barbara has issues". She saw this beautiful, African American female with a good spirit and decided she wasn't going to like me, from day one.

Barbara oversees the benefits forms, logs them in, and sends them over to payroll. Every now and then, someone calls about their missing benefit form, which was not in the **Technology Official Personnel Folder (TOPF)**. I looked it up and saw who was the person who processed the benefit formed, it was Judy. I told Barbara it was Judy, and "she went into a rage".

I told this colleague how Barbara went into a rage about Judy's missing form. He said he had seen her before, in a "rage like that". I told Judy not to worry when Barbara goes on leave, "all hell will break out", and it did. The customers were calling in about their TSP forms were not processed. The customer said, "I gave it to Barbara six months ago". While she was on leave, Hannah got the key to Barbara's office, and looked in the upper cabinet and found the form and other forms not sent out. When she returned, that task was taken from her. Hannah said she was disappointed with Barbara, losing forms. Barbara told a colleague Mike, who came from (ALAF), don't listen to Alexis, when he asked for guidance on the process of the remedy ticket. I am surprised he didn't know the remedy ticket process, because that is how he got hired. Hannah was waiting on a remedy ticket Mike, had not answered. Hannah called (ALAF) and Mike answered. She asked him why he hasn't answered her remedy ticket yet? He said, "I will respond right now." Mike then asked her if she was hiring? Hannah asked him if he knew me, and she hired me. I was on the phone with this customer earlier, and she came to the customer service help desk to inquire about a person she talked to on the phone. I heard her voice, so I went up front, and the nurse said that's her. Barbara is on the other side of the door, looking at me, shaking her head, saying "don't help her since she doesn't know your name". Wow, she was serious. Crazy right? I step out and assist the nurse with her questions.

The second-year being at the JLC-Naval Affairs

This job entitles you to comprehension and common sense. This job is especially important, because the employment relationship is ultimately beneficial to the customer. The people who make up the workforce of an organization, industry, business sector, or economy. When a person doesn't get paid, that would lead to a chain reaction. This is why customer service has always been very personal to me. When I think about customers, I think about family. My responsibility became more than I was hired for, but I never complained. I was forced to take more calls and customer walk-ins, correcting my colleague's work and supervisor's mistakes. When the supervisor has an appointment with the customer, she disappears, then I would always cover for her. One day, I asked Hannah, why can't my colleagues correct their own mistakes? She never answered. I am knowledgeable and skilled, and able to respond to customers' problems. This is why she takes advantage of me.

MY SUPERVISORS HANNAH BROWN THOUGHT PROCESS

When Chief Hack came on board, Hannah had one of the colleagues, Lowell, process his relocation bonus. The colleague incorrectly processed the relocation bonus and was not able to fix it. I told Lowell, I can help him with that. Hannah said, the customers come first. "Go figure that", coming from somebody who does not put the customer first. Chief Hack continues to inquire about his bonus, which hasn't been processed. I told Hannah I would work on Chief Hack's bonus. Hannah said he can wait, other people's pay comes first. I worked on it, because of her mindset. I reached out to my girlfriend Cynthia, in Palo Alto, California, for assistance. I submitted it to the UCIT-9 to delete it in (ALAP), and reprocess it. Chief Hack still complained his relocation bonus was off about $2.75.

I sent back the remedy ticket, asking if the system correctly calculated the Chief Bonus? When he left my desk, he was still not satisfied. I guess $2.75 is a lot? Crazy right?

I was hired for HR benefits, but yet the payroll office would send the customers to me when they can't explain their pay and retroactive payment.

HANNAH BROWN REFUSES TO DO HER JOB AND UPPER MANAGEMENT COULDN'T MAKE HER

Chief Hack has asked Hannah to correct the employees' records, and she refuses to. On this particular day, the Chief came to Hannah's office and asked her if she corrected the employee's record? She said, no. Chief Hack was so mad he said to Hannah, "I see you are not going to do your job, so you do whatever you want and walk away." Okay, changing roles. If she were an African American supervisor, what would have happened? Do you think she would still be working there? No. After Chief Hack left, I walked into Hannah's office and asked her if she had a minute? She said yes, with all smiles. She started telling me what Chief Hack had said. I told her "I overheard everything". My cubicle is about seven feet away from her office.

Helping my supervisor Hannah Brown

One day, I told Hannah this is what "we will do". We are going in your office, lock the door, and don't answer the phone to anyone. It works for about 20 minutes, then she answered the phone. There was a knock at the door, she told me to see who that is? I think she told the colleagues to knock on the door. One day, Hannah stood outside my cubicle, with Mike trying to get their story together. What lied they were, going to tell Chief Hack. I stepped outside of my cubes and looked at them. They lifted and went outside, plotted and lying all the time.

Remembering seeing Hannah, sad staring at her computer monitor

Hannah was sitting at her desk, staring at her monitor. I asked her what was wrong with her? She showed me an email of a high-level effectual, who works at the (JLC)-Headquarters in Washington D.C. This person sent her a nasty and derogatory email. It said something like this: "You" stupid, ignorant fool, do you want me to come down there and print out your work and read it to you?" Do your job. I told her I would send that email back, "saying that person a thing or two". Hannah said, no, because this is coming from Headquarters in D.C. This lady at the headquarters copied this email to the names of many people in Headquarters in D.C. She then soon retired. When I filed an EEO complaint against Hannah for giving me a bad reference, I asked for her to be removed as a supervisor? This is what Hannah wanted. She has been sounding the alarm for years, that she didn't want to be a supervisor. She asked the Chief if she stepped down, could she keep her salary? After my filing, they removed her and promoted her to a GS-12.

Allowing an employee Tina to place me on a checklist to undermine me

My colleague, Tina, told Hannah that I was making errors on the benefit forms I was submitting. This was not true. These were the same two African American ladies with all that chaos with the forms. (Tina and Barbara). Tina told Hannah that I needed to start submitting a checklist sheet, with the benefit forms, to ensure they were filled out correctly. I asked Hannah, why am I the only one submitting the benefit check sheet? She said she will tell the others they have to. I had to submit this benefit check sheet, if not Hannah will not release the customers' forms to process. Hannah said, at one point, she didn't understand why Tina forced Alexis to submit this form, because she didn't see anything wrong with my work. Crazy right? Hannah is my supervisor, and Tina is my colleague. "Go figure that". From day one, I have been fixing their errors and mistakes. I've never made mistakes, because I'm careful in what I do. Tina's duty was to accept my work, with the checklist forms, and upload them to the **Technology Official Personnel Folder (TOPF)**. After Hannah processed the form and release it. This system allows each customer to access all their benefits forms as soon as they are uploaded to the (TOPF). Before she left, she told me to "get the f_ _k out of her cubical" and it was loud in front of our colleagues. I was not the only one she would curse out. A few days later, she informs me if she goes off on me, It's the medication she's on. I told the Chief, and to this day, "I have not received an apology for the offensive language," she said to me and others. When Tina left, Hannah went into her office and discovered Tina had not uploaded any of my forms. The customer's forms were never uploaded to the (TOPF). For this reason, customers kept calling me about their benefits forms, because Tina never uploaded them. "Go figure that".

RACIAL DISCRIMINATION INTERNAL AND EXTERNAL EMPLOYEES AND CUSTOMERS

When I went on leave, many African Americans, internal and external, especially customers, complained about Judy, who works in the office with me. Customers said they waited, until I returned from leave, to assist them with their pay. The customer looked at me, then I intervened and told Judy I could help. I have witnessed Judy not wanting to help the customers, or not give the information, to other African American customers. "She was getting nasty with them", I told the customer to come to my desk. Judy got mad and left the room. "I didn't care". I can't stand there, letting people miss treated. She told Hannah "anything and everything she could think of about me". I still smiled at her. Because I know that "her reaction does not reflect me". Judy asked me to meet her after work at her favorite restaurant downtown. Judy refused to give me her phone number if I got lost. I know most people would have said, "I wouldn't have gone." I am quick to forgive, but I don't forget. This was not the first time. I lived four minutes from downtown. She wanted to get information on the status of my EEO case, to share it with my previous supervisor, Hannah. "I ignored her emails". This was the end of our working relationship, and she stopped emailing me. Judy treated me horribly. Sometimes, I "felt the prejudice in her". I just didn't go there, "I pretend". She always had a sweet tooth. When I went to the store, I always brought her something back. But when I asked her, "she had a difficult time saying yes". It would be something, simple as a celery. This heifer "had a stingy attitude". When I went to the store, I stopped bringing her stuff back. We went everywhere together, like meetings or events, and had a nice time. We were good, outside the office. I had to pretend, knowing how she felt about me, because we shared office space.

"HANNAH'S SUPERVISOR" WANDA HATED ME

Wanda never spoke to me in the three years while she worked for John Long Corporation (JLC). That didn't bother me, at least I know where we stand". There were times when she tried to take me down.

One time, she tried to place me on leave without pay (LWOP) status. On another occasion, she will not acknowledge that a customer sent me an email about me, doing a "good job, well done!"

1. In September 2015, I sat at my desk at 8:34 a.m., according to the time on my computer. Hannah has a policy that if you are late, you can make it up at the end of your shift. Hannah's Supervisor, Wanda, told her secretary, Sue, to call Alexis and tell her I saw her come in at 8:40 a.m., and she needed to put in a leave slip. If she doesn't put in a leave slip, she will place you on LWOP. I sent Wanda an email showing her, when she saw me, I had already logged into my computer, and was heading to Judy's desk to give her a package. She said I could have altered the email. Wanda told Sue to tell me, that's not true, put in a leave slip, or else I will place her on LWOP.

2. In July 2015, a doctor at the (JLC) hospital sent my 2nd level supervisor, Wanda, an email. Dr. Wright told her how he appreciated my assistance in helping him resolve his problem with FEHB resolution. I researched how to get a medication approved by calling the Office of Personnel Management (OPM) resolution. Dr. Wright asked me, did I see the email of appreciation he sent to Wanda? I said, no. He said he sent it to this supervisor, Wanda, whose name you gave me, who was responsible for sending out the kudos! I asked Wanda, did she

receive an e-mail from Dr. Wright? She said, no. Wanda continues to say she hasn't received the email. Dr. Wright sent me the email he sent Wanda. She replied to his email, saying "thank you". Wanda usually sends everyone an e-mail sharing their "kudos" with all employees.

3. In October 2016, Wanda told another supervisor, Chuck, to put me on LWOP, because I didn't call in. That morning, when I woke up and my car was towed, I sent an email to Chief Hack, and his secretary Sue, telling him that my car was towed. Hannah was out of office, and her supervisor Wanda was removed from her job. She was then detailed to the Equal Employment Opportunity office to answer the phone only. I am pretty sure she did more than that, like "looking at my EEO case". Someone filed an EEO complaint against Wanda, so she was no longer working under Chief Hack. In his absence, Chief Hack appointed Chuck to oversee his duties. Wanda was unaware of me sending an email, and speaking to Chief Hack secretary Sue. As soon as Chuck saw the email, I sent it two hours before the time expired, and told him I spoke to the secretary. He said: "Don't worry. I am glad Wanda left, because she was treating African Americans unfairly. Several of her employees were invited to a party at Wanda's house. It was told Wanda had pictures offensive to African-Americans.

GIVEN EMPLOYEES PROMOTION FOR NOT WORKING AND ON THE SPOT, CASH AWARD TO KEEP QUIET KAREN, SAM, AND LOWELL

Sam was always losing customer's benefit forms, so Hannah took away his duties. The colleagues asked, "What will he do now?" Sam and Lowell don't take many customer calls, and are gone from their desk for many hours. Karen that sits on the helpdesk would transfer a call to Sam or Lowell, and they would "literally" look at the phone and will not answer it. I have stood there and witnessed it. If they don't answer the call, Karen would transfer the calls to me, or Judy. If the boys didn't want to answer the calls today, Hannah would lie about why they shouldn't answer the phone today. Remember Judy, who told me, "Hannah like boys." She would make the females work, and the males would do whatever they wanted.

Sometimes, if Karen gets a call and she's by herself on the help desk, she would ask me to assist her, directing the calls to the right person. Karen was awarded a cash award twice within four months, and the boys were promoted.

PERFORMANCE RATING

How can two employees' performance ratings be the same? One is a clerk who answers the customer service help desk all day, and when it's slow, the supervisor will have her do a little filling. The other person is an HR assistant that processes benefits, counsels employees, who are separating, retired, and new hire, etc. We both received the highest rating you can get, which is outstanding; $1000-achievement levels for all elements. Four months later, Karen received an additional $600. She was still answering calls to the helpdesk and filing a little. When I received my last Performance rating-Outstanding, it was supposed to be $1000, but I received a check in the mail for $400. I called Hannah and was unable to reach her. "Go figure that". I talked to Tina, and she said they didn't receive the funding they expected. Is that truly the real reason, or after I left they decided to give me less? Hannah is still mad at me because I left. "Slavery is over". Everyone wondered, "how in the world" did Sam and Lowell receive a promotion without fulfilling their duties? Did I mention Hannah was the supervisor? "Corruption" This will be explained later.

IT LIES IN SCANDAL AND CORRUPTION

WHEN I WAS TOLD THAT I WAS MOVING OVER TO TRAILER-22

When I was told my colleague, Judy, and I were moving to trailer-22, I was happy. Hannah was so unhappy. She told me and others, "we should protest not to go there." I asked her why? She said they are angry people, and they are always cursing over there. I was glad to move, because the little boys "have filthy mouths". It gets so overwhelming, that I went outside to get some air. I couldn't concentrate on my work, so I decided to tell Hannah. Hannah called them, one by one in her office. Listen to this, you tell the supervisor your colleagues used the "F_ _k" word every minute." The outcome was, she told them to say, "Buck". Instead, I'm sitting in my cubicle, and they're standing outside my cubicle saying "Buck, Buck, Buck". She allowed them to disrespect other colleagues, so "they disrespected her". Sometimes people in the other part of the trailer come and tell them to "knock it off". Lowell has gone off on Hannah and "she wouldn't say anything". She just goes back to her office. One of the senior colleagues, Ray, stepped up in Lowell's face and said, "Hey". You don't talk to your supervisor like that, it's disrespectful. "You need to apologize to her". She tells them to disrespect, Chief Hack, when he makes her mad. They started chanting and talking about his bowtie until someone came and said, "knock it off". This is the kind of relationship she has with these boys.

Filing an EEO compliant in February 2016 on my supervisor

I have the right to file an EEO complaint, because no one is above the law.

If I hadn't, I would have never gotten out of there. I always felt she gave me a bad reference, but could never prove it until one day, it came back "in a full circle".

In February 2016, Hannah (JLC)-Naval Affairs, Florida, gave me an unfavorable reference to the selected officer for a position I applied for. This was a Financial Supervisor Analyst position as GS 09/11, with an incentive of $5,000 if I accepted the job.

I was highly qualified and the only person on the cert. The selected officer interviewed me with a panel of other people, including the employee Paul, who set up the interview for the job. My girlfriend Cynthia, who worked for me at (ALAF) in Indianapolis, Indiana, told me to apply for the job. Cynthia is now working for Palo Alto, CA. I was excited because my son attended school in California. After the interview, I asked the selected officer Ken, how is the weather? He said, "I will tell you how the weather is, it's like South Carolina." I wondered why he said, S.C. He said I was stationed in South Carolina. I said, "Do you know my family?" He said, yes. I was hired for my knowledge and skill in payroll, and that interacts with the ability to transfer into the Human Resource office. Once the interview was over, I received an email from Paul, who set up the interview, asking how do you think you did? I said I did okay, considering they allowed me to blab on. Paul said, "You did not disappoint me". Paul said, "Get ready to move" and asked me when I could start? I still have that email Paul sent me. Ken called and said, Alexis, "everything checks out", but I need to talk to your supervisor, Hannah. He said he is going on vacation, but he needs to finalize this before he leaves. I transferred him to Hannah, but she was not in the office. I called Hannah's cell phone. She told me to give Ken her cell phone number because she was out of the office. The next week, I called the Human Resource specialist in Palo Alto, California, who was responsible for processing my paperwork. The customer service assistant, Toni, told me the name of the HR Specialist working on my paperwork, Hebert Joseph Ozark. Before Toni transferred the call, he talked to Joseph. He told Toni to tell me he would call me in a few days. At the end of the week, I called back. The same person Toni, who answers the customer service help desk, said to me, Joseph hadn't called you back?

I said, no. He said, "hold on". He called Joseph, and came back and told me to leave a message. I left a voice message on Hebert Joseph Ozark's phone. I called back another time, and a lady answered the customer service help desk. She looked up the name, to see who was processing my paperwork. She said it was Hebert Joseph Ozark, then she said let me transfer you. If you call three times, "you can't get the same name wrong three times". When I returned to trailer-4, Karen at the help desk said she took a call for me, and the call came back, and he asked to speak to your supervisor Hannah. Karen said it was HR from Palo Alto, California. Karen said she went to Hannah's office when she transferred the call. I asked Karen if she stayed in Hannah's office the whole time? She said, no.

BAD REFERENCE

Later that week, I went to Hannah's office to start going over the employees' pay records.

Hannah asked me if the selected officer, Ken, called me yet? She told me to call him, because he told her he was going to hire me.

I ask Hannah what kind of questions he asks her? He asked if you were a good worker, and I said yes. I ask her, what else he asks you? Hannah said, "I told him you have issues, and if you want her, you will be taking her off my hands," I said. What? Did you say that? Hannah said no, I'm kidding. I said, what else did he ask you? The selected officer, Ken, asked if I would rehire you if you returned? I told him yes.

I texted my girlfriend at Palo Alto, California, who encouraged me to apply for the supervisor's payroll position. Cynthia said they haven't called you yet? She said, they like you and hired you. Cynthia said, "I am going to the all-hands meeting and see what's going on". She returned and said the selected officer, Ken, was not back from leave. She said the HR specialist Joseph, who was working on your paperwork, went on leave. The same name is Human Resources Specialist Hebert Joseph Ozark.

Cynthia said, "Let me call you back, I will check with someone else." When she returned, she said they told her to tell Alexis, that Hannah gave her a bad reference. I told Cynthia she was lying, and she said, I'm not. She said Paul, who sat up, the interview, said her supervisor, Hannah, gave her a bad reference.

Cynthia then said they told her what Hannah said, "You have issues, and if you want her, you will be taking her off my hands." That's when I knew Cynthia wasn't lying. That was a confirmation. She also said when they told her she was on the speakerphone, she said, it anyway. Cynthia said, the people in the room said, "Wow. I hung up the phone and wandered around in disbelief and anger.

I went to the store and bought myself a bottle of wine. I had a few drinks and then called Hannah at home. It irritates me when somebody flat-out lies in your face. I have a very low tolerance for this behavior. I asked her if she gave me a bad reference? She said, no. I asked Hannah, do she remember the conversation we had in her office, about what kind of questions Ken asked you? She said, yes. Why? I ask her, does she remember saying this, "that I have issues, and if you want her, you will be taking her off my hands"? Then I said, "Did you say that?" Then you said I was just kidding, I didn't tell Ken that. I said the agency said you gave me a bad reference and quoted the same thing you said you didn't say. Hannah said, I said it to you, but not to the agency. I asked her, "How would they know what you said?" She said, "I didn't know". Hannah said she will talk to the Chief tomorrow about this. We just ended the conversation on that note. "She's a pathological liar".

When I process the customer benefits for Hannah to release, she refuses to release them. Hannah stopped releasing my work. I had to cancel all actions I processed, because it would create a pay problem. One day, she was leaving, and she still refused to release the customers' benefits in the system. I texted Hannah on the message chat and started telling her off. I told her this is not about her, "it's about the customers, you failing". Then Judy said, Hannah, is staying. She released all my documents into the system.

I started having an anxiety attack. I couldn't stay in the building, I kept going outside to breathe. Luckily, I had a window in my office next to my desk. The doctor prescribed me medication for anxiety. I prayed about everything before filing an EEO complaint against my supervisor, Hannah, for giving me an unfavorable reference. As soon as I did it, "I felt much better". "I wanted her to feel the same way I felt". But that was not to be. I felt trapped, and if I hadn't filed an EEO, I would have never gotten out of there.

When you file an EEO complaint, the agencies frown on you. Abuse of authority.

What happened in the Equal Employment Opportunity case

I requested Hannah be removed when I filed an Equal Employment Opportunity Complaint against her for giving me a bad reference. They removed her and gave her a promotion to a GS-12.

The EEO investigator, Betty, interviewed the employees at the JLC-Gainesville facilities. Some employees resigned. When the EEO investigated the employees at the Palo Alto, California facilities, she did not place their statement in the Report of Investigation (ROI). "She kept telling me it was in there". "I kept telling her it's not". Then she said, when I go to the hearing, "ask the judge to give it to you". "What the heck". So now, the judge is doing the investigator Betty's job, "is that how it works?" Corruption.

The attorney, Patrice Washington for the John Long Corporation Gainesville, FL, sent me a letter to discuss a settlement in May 2017. I gave her my offer and she said she will go back to the agency and debate it.

Letter of Settlement May 2017

Ms. Montgomery

I have been assigned to manage this case on behalf of John Munson M.D. Secretary, Office of National War Affairs, hereinafter the Agency. Please direct any communication about this matter to me. At this time, I would like to discuss any settlement possibilities that you may suggest. Please contact me, in writing, at the address shown above so we may start these discussions. Please note that you have the option to by-passing the Equal Employment Opportunity Commission hearing process and proceeding directly to the issuance of the Final Agency Decision (FAD) from the office of Employment Discrimination Complaint Adjudication (OEDCA) which my expedite a decision on your case.

If you have any questions, please feel free to contact me.
Sincerely
Patrice Washington, Staff Attorney

At the hearing in January 2018, (JLC)-War Affairs attorney Patrice Washington told the judge she was going to settle with me, until I decided to obtain a representative. Then settlement was off the table. I told the judge that I did not receive the employee's statements from Palo Alto, CA. It was not included in the Investigation Report (ROI). I requested the statement from the attorney, Ms. Washington, and never received it. In September 2020, I filed a Civil Action to settle this case. A congressional request was sent to attorney Patrice Washington to request the employee's statement, but no response. The Representative who sent the congressional asked me, four months later, have I received the employees statement from Patrice Washington? I said, no. The agency attorney refuses to cooperate. The evidence is there, they just wish this African-American girl would disappear. This order came from the highest top-level in Headquarters, Washington D.C. I received a phone call out of the blue, that the Director from (JLC)-War Affairs, in Headquarter, was leaving. I had requested he be removed, because he is the decision-maker. Three months later, I asked, did he leave? They said, no. I guess he was making a "statement that he is above the law". Abuse of Authority.

"He thinks black lives don't matter."

MY LAST DAY

On my last day, November 2016, Hannah called me into her office to go over my performance appraisal. The rating is as follows: outstanding, excellent, fully, etc. Hannah rated me excellent and said she struggled with this rating, had no choice but to give it to me. She said HR Staffing told her that every time they asked me to do something, I said, no. "I told her she was lying". She also refuses to put in the appraisal that I utilized the (ALAF), remedy system. I told her I was going to sign my appraisal, but I would write below it, "I do not agree." That "heifer snatched the pen from my hand" and made the changes. She changed it to "Outstanding" and added my duties, and gave me a copy of my performance appraisal. Before I left, I just had to say it, "AGAIN", I told her, "She gave me a bad reference". Hannah yelled back at me, "no I said yes, you did". Then a colleague, Tina, came and escorted me from Hannah's office and walked me to the door. "That felt good." smile.

MICHAEL CONNECTION TO LEBRON JAMES

It's about a sweet little boy having dreams. He doesn't know why he is having these dreams and what they meant. Michael was about five years old on a Sunday morning in Charleston, S.C. I was driving down Riverside Avenue, when Michael said, "Grandma came to me last night". I was so shocked when he said that. He was only two years old, when he laid on her chest, before she passed away. I took a deep breath and said, what did she say? He said she said, "Hello" Michael. Then I asked, "did she have her legs and arm?" He said, yes. My mother lost her legs, and an arm from diabetes. She died of a broken heart, the death of her son Anderson Williams. I asked Michael, what she was wearing? He described a "house dress she wore back then". I was at odds when he said that. Then I asked him where I was?

He said, "You were behind me". I said, "What did I say?" "He said, she yelled out your name, saying "Alexis" if you don't get in this house. That was the tone of my mother's voice when she called us into the house when it was getting dark.

That took me back. It was surreal. I got quiet and continued to drive. I was at odds. As he continued to get older, he would get up some morning saying, "Mommy, I had another dream". I told Michael to write it down, or sometimes I would write it for him. As a teenager, his gift became more advanced and powerful. He started telling people who would win the NFL or NBA games. In one incident, when I dropped Michael off at the barbershop, he told the guys in the barbershop who would win the game.One day, I looked around in his bedroom when I found a stack of papers, saying free haircuts. I asked Michael, "why are you giving free haircuts?" He said, because I told them who would win the game. I switched to another barber shop, I was afraid he might call the game wrong. Sports is a serious game, especially "when people are betting the games". Michael still has dreams, and tells people things. **When Lebron James won his first two NBA championships while playing for the Miami Heat, Michael predicted the Miami Heat would win in 2012 and 2013, and they did.** Just before the Miami Heat won the game, Michael wrote a song for Lebron James, recorded it, and posted it on YouTube.

During this time, Michael attended Full Sails University in Orlando, Florida. Lebron's photographer also attended Full Sails. Michael gave his photographer the CD he made for Lebron James, not sure if he ever received the CD. **During the 2018 Super Bowl, when the Philadelphia Eagles beat the New England Patriots, Michael told me that Philadelphia would win the Super Bowl.** I sent an email to the people at (EWFT), who were Patriot fans, that Philadelphia would win the Super Bowl. He predicted the score would be between 7 and 11. I asked him, what does that mean? He said he doesn't know, "it just came into his head like that". The score was 44 for Philadelphia and 33 for the Patriot, subtract, 44-33 it was in the range. I was able to understand and analyze Michael's dreams, because I'm gifted. In the beginning, I didn't want him to talk about his dreams. I told him that people might not understand it. How do you know "as a parent that God chose Michael?" This is a spiritual gift of the heavenly father.

Joel 2:28 KJV. God said it shall come to pass afterward, that I will pour out my spirit upon all flesh; and your sons and your daughters shall prophesy, your old men shall dream, dream, your young men shall see the vision.

My mother told my sister to take care of Michael and Alexis on her dying bed. My mother was also gifted, perhaps she saw Michael and my vision. In 2010, I went through something when I worked for Accounting Lorton and Firm (ALAF) and thought about leaving the government. I was so pissed at them, I decided to "channel my energy by writing things down". One day, a whisper came to my ear to write a book about Michael's dreams. I decided to collect all his dreams and published "A Whisper to A Child's Ears from God" 100% faith.

ASKING GOD, A QUESTION AND RECEIVING THE ANSWER THAT MOMENT OR THE NEXT DAY "OMG"

- When I go on road trips, I have always prayed about it. I say, dear God, I'm going on a road trip to Atlanta, GA. Will I have car problems? Normally, I have the dream before, getting on the road trip if I encounter any problems with the car. In the dream, God showed me the back tire, flat. I had to replace it before I got on the road.

- On the next road trip, I prayed again. In the dream, it said something going to happen with my tires again. A week before I left, I heard a clone noise in front of my car. It was the wheel bearing. This was crucial. Thank you, Lord.

- In June 2013, I was going on yet another road trip. I pray about it. In the dream, God showed me my car was steaming, from under the hood. I remember "being frightened in the dream". It was time for me to get on the road. I thought about the dream and said nothing hasn't happened. "So, I'm going on". I went to Alabama to visit my sister. I was driving back from Alabama, and went up a tall, steep hill on the highway. Then I smelled something burning, and "saw the steam coming out of the car". It was 5:00 a.m. I was so scared that I got off the highway, and drove into the empty, Walmart parking lot. I lifted the hood-up and saw nothing burning. I drove around Walmart, parking lot and couldn't find anything burning. I proceeded onto the highway, and nothing happened. After driving, I realized I was driving a car with a stick shift, and had it in the wrong gear, going up a hill. I was burning the clutch, that's why it smelled. "Can you believe that?" God probably had a good laugh, looking down at me in panic. "He is my protector". Thank you, Lord.

- I had this dream when I lived in Charleston, S.C., in 2004. My son was about six years old. Every night, I went into his room and prayed with him. I closed my eyes and started praying, then a lot of money fell from the sky in my hands. It was "brand new money", falling into my hands. I was so frightened, I opened my eyes. I said, to myself, "what was that?" I waited for a moment and began praying again. "The same thing happened again". I opened my eyes, and was a little confused, about, "why was brand new money falling out of the sky in my hands?" I waited for about ten minutes, closed my eyes, and started praying again. "This time it was all dark". I went to my bedroom, sat down, and tried to make sense of it. I'll wait until it comes to pass. I remember asking God, "If this is mine?" "I can definitely, use it now".

- This dream occurred when I lived in Indianapolis, Indiana, in 2011. In the dream, I was in the Navy Federal (NFCU). I was at the counter, asking the teller how much money I had in my savings account. The clerk pulled up my account and said hold on, "it's going to take some time". I remember my sister came to the door of (NFCU), I went over to talk to her. I asked her in the dream, where are you going? She said she was going to California to build a house. She left, and I returned to the counter, to wait for the clerk. I asked (NFCU) how much money do I have in my account? This is what the clerk said. "It's a lot, I can't count it". The next thing I said, give me $60.00. I remember that "in real-time", I had borrowed and owed my sister $60.00. Maybe this was a way God told me "This dream will come true".

- I had a conversation with an in-law about a family member and told her not to say anything. After time, I felt she may have told that family member. I love her with a smile and wonder if she has spoken of it. I kept feeling this feeling in my heart. I got on my knees and prayed. I said, dear God, I told my in-law something, please take this sense of feeling from my heart. As soon as I finished praying, when I got up, "a voice said you will know". "I said back to the voice, how?" The next thing it said was daunting. The voice said, "she will tell on herself". I was a little confused. Two days later, I spoke to my in-law on the phone, and she said she talked to that family member about it. OMG, I didn't tell you to tell her. She said, "I thought you did". I told her no, but it was okay. I was amazed by the transparency.

- When I lived in San Diego, California, my family came to visit me. We decided to go to Disneyland and Universal Studios. I went to the Marino Navy base to settle my travels. All travel must be in no later than 2:00 p.m., or it wouldn't be processed the next day. Then it takes two to three business days for the processing, before the deposit. I got there after 2:00 p.m. When I got home, I mumbled, "I wish I had enough money to splurge, at the fun parks." That night, I had a dream that $1,500.68 was deposited in my bank account. The next morning, I woke up at 6:00 a.m. and called NFCU. The automated system said, "You have $1,500.68 deposited in your checking account. It was exactly the amount I dreamed of. Wow, it was surreal.

Economical Warfare fighter training (EWFT) Base Virginia

My first Supervisor Mr. Carter

On the first day, I arrived at the HR orientation at 8: 30 a.m. I knocked at the back door of the training room, that's locked. The HR specialist Alexander walked over to open the door and stopped, with a question from the HR lady asking, if I was on time? Short female, other than African American. It was about me, being occasionally five minutes late, at my last job. This agency "singles me out from day one, when I arrived". I pretend this didn't just happen. After the orientation, I went to Economical Warfare Fighter Training (EWFT), to meet my supervisor, Mr. Carter. I thank him for selecting me, "he proclaims, a man of good spirit". Mr. Carter told me they have Bible studies in the conference room on Tuesdays, at noon, and I was welcome to come. Mr. Carter said, because I didn't have access to the system, this would be a good time to take some leave if needed. Mr. Carter also said you don't have to rush back from lunch or break on time. Just check-in when you returned. The payroll CSR, Michelle, was teleworking in Florida. She reached out to me and welcomed me on board. I went about my everyday business for about a month, until Mr. Carter called me into the office, and told me that I was returning from lunch and breaks late. I went back to my desk and said to myself, "what just happened". What did Mr. Carter mean? When he asks me if I want him to change my schedule, it will still be a regular work schedule. There was a young lady on-site as the CSR, her name is Janice. She trained me in Data Personnel System Analyst Collection (DPSAC), before she left.

I just listened to Janice and didn't comment because I was new to the job, and didn't know her. Janice said she sat at Director, Connie Thurmond's desk, and assisted her with the phone calls. Janice reminded me of our supervisor, Mr. Carter's behavior toward her again. Once Janice returned to her desk, I asked SSgt Green, why is there any work? He said, "it is political". SSgt Green said, to ask Janice to take you to the parking lot, and explain it to you. Janice took me to the parking lot and said yes, "there's no work". Janice said you should do a lot of training to stay busy, and if you want to go to school, this would be the time to go. Janice said that's why she is sitting at Director Connie's desk. I didn't understand Janice's relationship with Mr. Carter. At one point, she was not sure what Mr. Carter wanted, her to train me, on next. She asked Mr. Carter what he wanted, Alexis trained on next? After he told her. The strangest thing that happened next. Mr. Carter said, was daunting. He said, Ms. Montgomery, I'm going to take you to lunch. Janice got mad and said, "You never took me to lunch, and stormed back to her.", desk, and left me standing there. I went back to my desk and thought, "what just happened". Janice was always saying negative things about Mr. Carter, and "rolling her eyes". Janice reminded me, once more, about Mr. Carter and the CSR Michelle, behavior.

When I didn't respond, I could tell it was irritating her, and she said okay, and went back to her desk. As I said, I didn't understand her relationship with the supervisor. On her last day, she went to Applebee's restaurant, with her "supervisor", Mr. Carter. How can you go from hating your supervisor and sitting in front of him eating lunch? I asked Janice, how did lunch go? It was nice, she said. Janice received a promotion, gave me her phone number, and left. Mr. Carter started, retaliating against me. I called Janice and told her what Mr. Carter said to me. Janice said you think that's the end of it, I said, yes. She said, he will continue to mess with you. She said she filed an Equal Employment Opportunity complaint against Mr. Carter, changed her mind, and later went back and filed an EEO complaint against him. Janice said, if you need two people to back up your claim, you can use me, and another colleague, who was the CSR, before her. She said, Mr. Carter mistreated this colleague, and she went to Director Connie crying, and Director Connie said, "I'll talk to him." Janice said the colleague's husband received orders months later, and she left. She said, director Connie never did anything about it. When it comes to African Americans "making wrong right", she doesn't "give a ram about anyone except herself". Janice had a friend I just met, worked upstairs, and will transition downstairs as the director's Connie secretary, Chris. I went upstairs with Chris to help her collect the rest of her items from her old desk.

When Chris got to her desk, her things were moved. She became irritated, a little rattled, that someone had moved her things. Chris asks the two ladies, sat next to her desk, if they knew where her things were. We found them in another selection. When I saw what it was, "I said to myself, she got mad over this." One day, she came to me and told me that Janice wanted to meet us for lunch at the club. I said, okay. We went to the club for lunch and waited for Janice, she never showed up. We were almost done with lunch, Chris said, "Let me call her," she didn't answer her phone. I decided to call her just before leaving, and she answered the phone. I said, I thought you were supposed to meet us at the club? I said, where are you? She said, "I am at home". I said I thought you were supposed to meet us at the club. She just laughs, that was weird. She never had an explanation why she didn't show. I paid for Chirs and I food, and went back to work. A week later, I asked Chris if she wanted to go to lunch sometime? She told me she was busy, and she didn't have time to go to lunch. I would always see her, going to lunch with some of my other colleagues. But never say, "hey Alexis, let's go to lunch". I noticed her loyalty was to director Connie, if she wanted to move up. At one point, I just didn't say anything to her. Let's just say I didn't go out of my way to speak. If she didn't speak, I didn't speak. I have never acted like this before, and it has nothing to do with going to lunch. I knew it was not right, so I apologized to Chris. She said she wondered why I stopped talking to her? "Really" As my mother always says, "kill them with kindness".

SHARING-I remember running into a home girl on base, from my home town. Wow, small world. We decided to have lunch. After lunch, I offered to pay for her meal. She said, yes. We went back to work. After a while, she called to check on what's going on. "Let's keep it real, she's looking for some gossip". She asks how are things at work. "Pretend" I told her we could go to lunch, and talk about it. She said her finances were not good right now. I told her she didn't have to buy me lunch. She said, perhaps another time. I said, okay. One day, I went to the all-you-can-eat restaurant. She was surprised to see me, "She had two plates of food and she looked full." Every now and then she called, and I would say, everything was fine.

Going through the motion with my first supervisor Mr. Carter

Mr. Carter started to be more aggressive about me coming back from lunch and breaks. He wanted me to check in with him, when I returned from lunch and breaks. I see where this was going. I started sending an email to myself for three years, as I come and go. Mr. Carter sent me an e-mail saying I was late this morning, to put in a leave slip. I went into his office to dispute his claim on **Tuesday, August 1, 2017.** I said I got here around 8:00 a.m. I showed him my email that I send myself every morning. Then he said it must be **Wednesday, August 2, 2017.** I showed him a Wednesday email.

Then he asked me what day it was? I told him I'm not sure you have to figure it out, and walked out of his office. **Both emails show that I came in at 8:02 a.m.,** according to my computer, when I sat down. There were many times he accused me of being away from my desk longer than the norm. One day, he came into my area and said, "Hello Ms. Montgomery", how are you doing this morning, then left. Around 10:30 a.m., he entered the room again, had a joke with SSgt Green, and left. Mr. Carter came back at about 2:00 p.m. and said, Ms. Montgomery, I have not seen you all day. I try to refresh his memory by asking him if he remembers coming in this morning, joking with SSgt Green? He said, no. Have you ever had someone who didn't want to train you and gave you false information? Mr. Carter told SSgt Green to train me on how they process accounting, and he frowned. When I asked him a question, he ignored me. After asking, SSgt Green, for help, and no response. I went to Mr. Carter and told him, SSgt Green is not answering my questions. He called SSgt Green to his office, and when SSgt Green returned to the room, he was mad. Director Connie gave Mr. Carter the go-ahead to give his employees 59 minutes. I was the only employee who had to stay until the end of my shift. One day, Mr. Carter said, Ms. Montgomery, I know it's seven minutes before your shift ends, but you can go. I said, "Gee, thanks". Mr. Carter called me into his office to go over my performance appraisal. Mr. Carter said he couldn't rate me, because I had not fulfilled the duties for which I was hired. Then he said, "Everybody is not your friend", at that moment, I knew who he was talking about. He said he couldn't rate me, because I had not fulfilled the duties for which I was hired. Then he said, "Everybody is not your friend", at that moment, I knew who he was talking about. There was a young lady with a schedule that ended, the same as Mr. Carter's schedule, at 6:00 p.m. Let's just call her Tamar, and refer to the group names I assigned. I confided in her how Mr. Carter treated me, she had been telling him everything I said. This broke what little relationship we had, as an employee and supervisor. The sad thing about it was, he didn't think he was treating me unfairly. Tamar told me everything about everyone in the building, and that is not in my spirit. It came a time when I wanted to put her in her place, and on the path of righteousness, from the negative things she said. I had to pretend with her. It's the spirit of the Lord, to accept everybody.

THE FIRST MSgt JAMES CALHOUN

MSgt James Calhoun was smart but immature, stupid, and doesn't have good leadership. He oversees the junior military. When Mr. Carter put me back on-off again on the accounting work, I would ask

MSgt Calhoun for assistance. He is knowledgeable in accounting, but my colleagues would say, if you have a question, Alexis, don't ask MSgt Calhoun for help. He was always running around, the office like a little boy, talking smack about me. My colleagues would say, don't ask MSgt Calhoun for assistance when you have a question. I knew he was talking, smack behind my back. But I am about "business", and I will not allow myself "to go there" when he has the information I needed. I would often say, "I can't believe these people are raising children". Some military troops would tease me, when 59 minutes are given, to my colleagues, and I would have to stay until the end of my shift. They would say, "You are not getting the 59 minutes because you were late". I would always ignore them, because "those comments are beneath me". Sgt Wilson went through a divorce and was given full custody of his child. He stayed behind when they were released for lunch, and asked for my advice. When Sgt Wilson returned from lunch, I went to his desk, and told him he needs to take his daughter to get counseling. MSgt Calhoun sits on the other side, of Sgt Wilson's desk, and overheard what I said. As soon as I sat down at my desk, MSgt Calhoun stood in front of Sgt Wilson's desk and was "very adamant about what he said". He said, "Your daughter doesn't need counseling, you are doing fine." I always say, "if you do not have common sense, don't get an education, because it's not going to help you". Respectfully. On New Year's Eve in 2017, I was standing over by Director Connie's office, talking to her secretary Chris and another colleague Ann. MSgt Calhoun "shouted out my name, asking where I was?" It was a skeleton crew in the office. The military troops were heading out when MSgt Calhoun called my name. I responded quietly. I knew he did not have common sense. The next thing that came out of his mouth, I was shocked. MSgt Calhoun said, "get your ass over here". I was embarrassed and humiliated in front of my peers. The sad thing was that his supervisor, LtCol Roy, was right there when he said it, and he said he didn't hear it. "He gave the order, and embraced the behavior". I asked LtCol Roy in a meeting, did he hear MSgt Calhoun tell me to "get my ass over here?" When Chris and Ann heard it, they placed their hand over their mouth with disbelief and shock.

When Chris and Ann were questioned by the Inspector General (IG), if they heard MSgt Calhoun, tell me to "get my ass over here?" They said they didn't hear him or "they didn't recall". "I knew slavery was over".

THE CORPORATE SOCIAL RESPONSIBILITY CSR MICHELLE

After I arrived, Michelle, Corporate Social Responsibility (CSR), contacted me and "welcome, me on board". Michelle has been teleworking and processing the payroll in Florida for three years when I arrived. She knew one of the colleagues, from (ALAF) Pensacola, to whom she was talking, on the phone. She said she knew my supervisor, Mr. Sutton, who is now the Director at the (ALAF) Cleveland, OH payroll office). She said, "Tell Mr. Sutton "Hello". Mr. Sutton said he didn't know her. A week later, Michelle called back and told me about the people I had to watch out for. Michelle said the supervisor, Mr. Putin, in the travel department, was always watching her. She said he watched her every time she left her desk. One day, she said he said something inappropriate to her, and she went off on him. Michelle said Mr. Carter had to call her husband to come and get her. She said I'm just letting you know that, and when I come to Virginia, I'll train you on some things in the Data Personnel System Analyst Collection (DPSAC). She said her husband received orders to Florida, and Director Connie told her to take her computer and process the payroll in Florida. I was told there were two employees before me, processing the payroll. One of them left because Director Connie allowed Mr. Carter to mistreat the employee. Mr. Carter told me Michelle should be working in the office at the Economic Warfare Fighter Training (EWFT) location. Especially when customers have a pay problem, or don't get paid on payday. Michelle uses her off-day, on payday Friday. When the new supervisor, Mr. Mudd, arrived, I had only remedy access for (ALAF). Mr. Mudd asked me to send a remedy ticket to (ALAF), requesting a special pay for the employee who didn't get paid. This requires me to ask the employee for their SSN, to submit a remedy ticket. Michelle and Mr. Mudd would not provide me with the employee's SSN, they told me the system doesn't use SSN (ALAF). This was one of "their strategies", denying me access, and not allowing me to do the job I was hired for. When my previous supervisor, Mr. Carter, accused me of being 15 minutes late, I went across the street to talk to a union representative and inquired about the 15 minutes. The Union representative said, "You don't know why you're being treated that way?" I said, no. The reason is that Michelle is processing the payroll in Florida, and it is illegal. They said it was supposed to be temporary. I said it sounds like they're trying to push me out. Michelle started sending me nasty emails. She treated me like she was the supervisor.

When I told Mr. Carter, he said I don't get involved with two women's problems. I said to him, would you say the same if Michelle sent the nasty emails to Mrs. Connie? He just "looked at me". Janice warned me before she left, Michelle sent her nasty emails, and Mr. Carter didn't say anything.

I said to him, would you say the same thing if she sent director Connie nasty emails? Janice warned me Michelle would send me nasty emails, because she sent them to her. I was sitting at my desk, and two male employees from upstairs came through the door from the vending machine area talking about Michelle. They were walking and talking about her as they passed my cubicle. The new employee said to the other employee, "Do you know Michelle talked to me nasty?" The other employee who worked for (EWFT) for a long time said, I know. The next thing he said was daunting. He said, "I will tell you something, Michelle did for me", and if you tell anyone, I swear I will deny it." I have an idea who they are, but because I have not seen their faces, it would be unfair to speculate. Ms. Connie, had Chris and Ann demonstrate how much conversation you can hear when you pass a person's cubicle. I was in one of the cubicles talking to a colleague who sits behind Gary's cubicle. Both walked one at a time, to the end of the door, and turned around, smiling as they demonstrated. They probably felt ridiculous, at least that's what their facial expression looks like. God has always allowed me to see people first, before they see me. Once I received my secret clearance, I thought I would receive work, but that was not the case. I sent Michelle an e-mail asking what she does every day as a CSR? "She ignored me." I had to file an Equal Employment Opportunity complaint against management to get work, "it became more difficult". Michelle and management interfered with the employee's schedule after I processed it. The results were that the employee did not receive a paycheck. My supervisor, Mr. Mudd, said it was my fault. I showed him the audit report, where Michelle was the last person to make changes to the employee schedule. He still said, it's my fault. Michelle and another administrator, Keith, kept changing the employee's records every pay week, without checking with me. I asked Mr. Mudd if he, or Michelle, made changes to the employee records? He said, no. Every pay period, they would deactivate this employee schedule, and I would ask if this employee is leaving? Mr. Mudd would say "not that I know of". This was another case of manipulation, accusing me of why an employee was not paid. This happened to another employee, who was on active duty reserve, and when she returned, the Human Resources Office (HR) did not process her paperwork on time. When the employee was not paid, Mr. Mudd and Director Connie told me it was my fault, even though I had proof of emails. I sent (ALAF) a remedy ticket to explain it to management in the remedy ticket. The remedy ticket was returned, explaining HR did not process the employee's paperwork on time. Management still said it was my fault. When I spoke to Inspector General Guy (IG). He told me, one week, they would see Michelle's name on the message board, the next week, Alexis's. Guy said it was confusing, because they did not know which (CSR) to call. Michelle took advantage of me, and tried to mislead the work processes.

I asked her to upload some documents needed to work in the Personnel System Analyst Collection (DPSAC) system, but she refused to submit the documents. I had to call San Diego and ask Administration, Keith, to upload my documents into the Personnel System Analyst Collection (DPSAC) system. He told me I did not have access yet, so he would upload them.

DIRECTOR CONNIE THURMOND

My supervisor, Mr. Carter, sat down and went over my responsibility when I arrived. He told me he would set up an appointment to meet Director Connie Thurmond, as standard protocol. I went to Director Connie's office, and we sat down and had a conversation. Ms. Connie welcomes me to **Economical Warfare Fighter Training (EWFT)**. She said, "Tell me a little about myself". Looking back, she had already known that I had filed an Equal Employment Opportunity complaint (EEO) on my previous job, before I arrived. Later, I found out Ms. Connie said she told Mr. Carter to let me go and come, as I did, since I didn't have access to the computer and couldn't take leave. **This was the start of a lavish scheme.** Ms. Connie says she has an open-door policy, but she didn't mean it. That's what everyone says, when they "leave and dread to go into her office". Ms. Connie allowed the supervisor, Mr. Putin, whom I whistleblower, to embarrass, humiliate and demean his employees in the travel department. Once you tell Director Connie, she tells the supervisors, and he/she retaliates against the person's name-dropped in the room. Ms. Connie instructed management and employees to disrespect me. She also told them not to talk to me when I returned from administrative leave. "What a heifer" When two employees were not paid, she sent me an e-mail asking why they were not paid? I sent her the audit report, showing that Michelle and Mr. Mudd went behind my back and changed the employee schedule. That heifer, Ms. Connie, sent me an email saying Mr. Mudd, and I agreed it was your fault.

This young lady went on active duty, and when she returned, Human Resources did not return her to duty on time, so she was not paid. I explained to Director Connie, what happened and sent her the remedy ticket from **Accounts Process Pay System (APPS) explaining.** Director Connie said it's my fault. The next thing Director Connie did was "unimaginable", she allowed a military member to lie on me. "I thought I'd seen it all". She and MSgt Kokum Wilson encourage the young Corporal Martin-Martinez to file an Equal Employment Opportunity complaint (EEO), against me. Ms. Connie came to my desk to remove me from my area, because the complaint was from Corporal

Martin-Martinez, who sat in the area. I didn't know who it was at the time. Ms. Connie tries to place me in the area where the supervisor, Mr. Putin, is located, on which I am the whistleblower. I told Ms. Connie, "I am not moving over in that area, because he doesn't like me". She said that's not true. She went back to her office. I kept calling and emailing General Stony, because he said he will protect me from any reprisal. "Here we are". Ms. Connie called me into her office and said she was sending me home on administrative leave, until further notice. She was "pissed off that her plan didn't work." She wanted to send me to the travel department, so Mr. Putin could torture me. In the first two weeks at home, I was stressed, but finally settled down. After two months, the investigator contacted me to hear my side of the story. I remember getting a call from Director Connie saying, "you can come back to work". She was not happy: "You can hear the coldness in her voice on the phone". When I returned to work, Ms. Connie and Mr. Mudd sat down and talked about where we go from here. The whole time, Ms. Connie was "pouting" because she did not succeed in permanently being removed, as General Stony requested. Ms. Connie told me she would not tolerate my behavior in the workplace. She asked Corporal Tim, the military troop standing next to Corporal Martin-Martinez, who saw it, how he felt, if it was done to him? Ms. Connie said Caporal Tim said he would be offended. Wow, I thought I was the victim because he clearly said he lied, it didn't offend him. Ms. Connie kept the drama going. This happened early on, I went to Ms. Connie's office to give her one of my books. First, I asked her if she was spiritual? She said the answer to your question is yes. She said I could not accept the book. During that time, I was standing there, and she was stroking my right arm up and down, and that was not the first time she was inappropriate. "Go figure that" I didn't say anything she may have thought; I didn't like it. "Joking". Then out of the blue, she said, "Have you gotten your security clearance?" I said, no. She said I will call and check on it, but she never did. Sometimes when she sees me coming in her direction, she would go the other way. Sometimes she comes to the sliding door and stands there enough that I couldn't see her, so she doesn't have to speak to me.

She would say "hello" to MSgt Kokum Wilson and wave to the military troops without letting me see her. I can see what she is doing as she stands at the edge of the door. I was surprised she was trying to interact with the troops, because she never showed kindness towards them, and their reactions toward her were, "back at you too". Wired right? She gives women a bad reputation in leadership. One day, it took its toll on me, how I was mistreated, and humiliated by Lt Col Roy and my superior, Mr. Mudd. I went to Ms. Connie's office to talk to her about my concerns. I stopped and talked to her secretary, Chris, about an appointment with Ms. Connie. I was very emotional. Ms. Connie heard me, turned her television down, and came out of her office. Ms. Connie stepped out of her office and walked two feet along the wall. She turned around, looked at me, and went back into her office. Her secretary Chris called me and said Director Connie was ready to see me. I told her my concerns about not being allowed to change my schedule, to have an RDO, day off, security clearance, and how it will affect my promotion. She said she would "set up a meeting" with LtCol Roy and your supervisor, Mr. Carter, and "I will be the mediator". She never attended the meeting. I went to my desk and came back, with a folder of things I wanted to address in the meeting. I tried to hand it to her, and then she drew back in her chair and said, "I don't want to see it". I placed in the folder what LtCol Roy and his wife Diana humiliated me at the Country Club Ball. She knew what was in the folder, so she tried to avoid it. I just "yelled out" that LtCol Roy's wife, Diana, told me to kiss her backside at the Country Club Ball. Then Ms. Connie said, what? "She said, "Are you sure?" She asked me twice. I said, yes. "Did I tell you she won an Academy Award for the best liar?" After returning to work, I told Mr. Carter how LtCol Roy and his wife, Diana, treated me at the Country Club Ball in 2017. Mr. Carter apologizes for LtCol Roy's behavior, saying he was there in the absence of Ms. Connie. She set up a meeting with my supervisor, Mr. Carter, and LtCol Roy, and she didn't show up. **'A Ella no le importaba un carajo' in English, "she didn't give a damn."** This order of how to treat me came from the highest level, the highest D.C. I filed a congressional asking for answers from Director Connie: why am I not receiving work, and if or when will I receive my promotion? Director Connie responded to the Congressional, telling me to file a grievance if that is what I wish to do. I still don't know why I'm being treated in this way, and why I have to file a grievance. The Equal Employment Opportunity investigator asked Director Connie if she set up a meeting for LtCol Roy, Mr. Carter, and me in January 2018?

She lied and said she didn't set up a meeting for me to meet with the two supervisors. Ms. Connie loves to keep an eye on me, I hardly ever leave my desk. One day, I went to the budget department to talk to a colleague, Faith, about her family member, with whom I was talking on the phone. As I approached the area down the way, Ms. Connie was standing in front of her office, talking to her secretary, Chris. As soon as I entered the budget area, Ms. Connie followed me shortly afterward and stood next to me.

I was just getting into the conversation with my colleague Faith, and we stopped talking to say hello to Ms. Connie. Faith and I went back to having the conversation, while she stood there. Then suddenly, Ms. Connie got mad and started walking away, "pointing her figure at Faith". Ms. Connie started saying to Faith, as she left, "You better have my five million dollars on my desk at the end of the day". Faith said what? Ms. Connie got angry just that quickly, repeated it, and left. I looked at Faith's face, as she tried to compose herself in disbelief, that Ms. Connie had just come into the room and humiliated her. It was all because she wasn't the center of attention. It was embarrassing. Remember she was in front of her office talking to her secretary, stopped talking to her, came down here to be nosy. I know this wasn't the first time Ms. Connie embarrassed Faith because she tried to leave Economical Warfare Fighter Training (EWFT) once, but "I told her it wanted, be a good time". "I keep telling people slavery is over". Director Connie has given the supervisors, and LtCol Roy, instructions on how to treat me. She also told the supervisors to tell the employees, not to talk to Alexis, when I returned. In 2018, I sent Ms. Connie an e-mail and copied her supervisors, telling her that I had a heart attack four months before I came to (EWFT) and was asthmatic. But again, she knew this before I got here. Ms. Connie was aware of MSgt Kokum Wilson spraying an unknown substance toward me, and that I had asthma. She ignored the warning. She knew, that LtCol Roy, the previous supervisor, Mr. Carter, and the new supervisor, Mr. Mudd, allowed other colleagues 59 minutes, and I had to stay until the end of my shift. She had the IT specialist go through my computer when I was not at work for no reason. Every time I returned to work, my files were mess-up, so I got tired of the bull crap. I stood up and said out loud, "I don't mind you looking in my computer, just put things back as they were". I would always have to call the "IT help desk" to fix my computer. I guess "Connie was trying to piss me off". She did. She treated me like a straight-up criminal. "As an African American, she violated my civil rights". I keep telling them that slavery is over. If you can't see or hear what was going on, I filed an EEO complaint against my former supervisor, so it's easy to hate an African-American. I wasn't the only African-American, some have come and gone and still feel the humiliation that was infringed on them. She lied and refused my security clearance. According to OPM, the secret clearance was "higher" than required to work for Economical Warfare Fighter Training (EWFT). OPM said, "I didn't need a background check". When I received my security clearance, it showed my background check was closed in 2013. Shortly after, I left Accounting Lorton and Frame (ALAF), in Indianapolis, Indiana. Director Connie said she would check in to my security clearance, but she never did. Abuse of Authority. She lied to OPM, made them part of her, abused authority, and corruption without them being aware of what was going on. . She never intended to give me my promotion from day one. That's why Janice warned me the first week I arrived. "All the signs were there". Director Connie took an oath of office.

I_____ do solemnly swear (or affirm) that I will support and defend the Constitution of the United States against all enemies, foreign and domestic; that I will bear true faith and allegiance to the same; and that I will obey the orders of the President of the United States and the orders of the officers appointed over me, according to regulations and the Uniform Code of Military Justice. So, help me God."

MEDITATION

I meditated for about two weeks on Director Connie. I wanted to stop being angry about how she treated me. One night I sat down and meditated, I could clearly see everything. I saw Director Connie leave her office, with a box full of things from her office. Once she got outside and stood by her vehicle, she waved goodbye.

MICHELLE OBAMA SAID WHEN THEY GO LOW YOU GO HIGH

LIEUTENANT COLONEL ROY

I remember asking Alexander, an HR Specialist, to ask the agency on two occasions if they would give me an advance so I wouldn't suffer a hardship. The agency said, no. I placed my household items in storage and accepted the position at Economical Warfare Fighter Training (EWFT), Base in Virginia. I did not remember being induced by LtCol Roy. I remember having a conversation on two occasions, when I first got to Economical Warfare Fighter Training (EWFT). One was about an up coming promotion. I felt he wanted to know if I had any insight into whether he would be promoted, and the other time it was about his family. I remember a strange spirit of turmoil, something about him. The next thing he started saying when he entered the room was. **"drain the swamp"**. It didn't take long "before his true colors came out". I took it like he was talking to me, but not indirectly in my face. "Coward." When he came in to talk to MSgt James Calhoun, who sat behind me, he would say **"drain the swamp"** and MSgt James Calhoun would **echo** behind him. **Drain the swamp** means: "to root out corruption", referring to me at that time. I didn't know it was about me, filing a prior Equal Employment Opportunity at my last agency. I hadn't been there long, and it was my first Christmas in Virginia in 2016. My colleague Tamar invited me to her house for Christmas dinner. I remember when I went back to work, she was still on leave. I went to her department to talk to her colleagues and said Tamar was nice, to invite me for Christmas dinner. It was five people in the room talking, and the room got quiet. LtCol Roy was standing center in the room, he put his head down. I learned that if you want to know something about somebody, just mention the person's name and say something sweet about them. "Watch their body language and facial expressions." We went shopping for a ball dress, and I was excited to go to the ball for the first time. On the evening of the Country Club Ball, I received a phone call from Tamar, telling me that she had changed the table arrangement, and would not be sitting at the assigned table with me. Tamar said she didn't want to sit at the table with LtCol Roy's wife, Diana, because all she talked about is her kids, and she was correct. That was the whole conversation. I would leave the table and come back, and she was still talking about them.

I remember asking Alexander, HR Specialist, to ask the agency on two occasions if they would give me an advance so I wouldn't suffer a hardship. The agency said, no. I placed my household items in storage and accepted the position at Economical Warfare Fighter Training (EWFT), Base in Virginia. I did not remember being induced by LtCol Roy. I remember having a conversation on two occasions, when I first arrived at Economical Warfare Fighter Training (EWFT). One was about an up-and-coming promotion. I felt he wanted to know if I had an insight into whether he would be promoted, and the other time it was about his family. I remember a strange spirit of turmoil, something about him. The next thing he started saying, when he entered the room, was. "drain the swamp". It didn't take long "before his true colors came out". I took it like he was talking to me, but not indirectly in my face. "Coward." When he came in to talk to MSgt James Calhoun, who sat behind me, he said "drain the swamp" and MSgt James Calhoun echoed behind him. Drain the swamp means: "to root out corruption", referring to me at that time. I didn't know it was about me, filing a prior Equal Employment Opportunity at my last agency. I hadn't been there long, and it was my first Christmas in Virginia in 2016. My colleague Tamar invited me to her house for Christmas dinner. I remember when I went back to work, she was still on leave. I went to her department to talk to her colleagues and said Tamar was nice, to invite me for Christmas dinner. It was five people in the room talking, and the room got quiet. LtCol Roy was standing center in the room, he put his head down. I learned that if you want to know something about someone, just mention the person's name and say something sweet about them. "Watch their body language and facial expressions." We went shopping for a ball dress, and I was excited to go to the ball for the first time. On the evening of the Country Club Ball. I received a phone call from Tamar, telling me that she had changed the table arrangement, and would not be sitting at the assigned table with me. Tamar said she didn't want to sit at the table with LtCol Roy's wife, Diana, because all she talked about was her kids, and she was right. That was the whole conversation. I would leave the table and come back, and she was still talking about them.

THE COUNTRY CLUB BALL

When I arrived at the Country Club Ball in November 2017, Major Smith's wife, Patricia, and another colleague Pam were already sitting at the table. Tamar invited me to a table in the back of the ballroom, but when I got back there, she said the seat was no longer available. I did not know Pam, who was sitting at the table, she worked in the travel department. Things were going well, having fun with Major Smith and his wife, Patricia, until LtCol Roy and his wife, Diana, arrived. LtCol Roy started introducing his wife, Diana, to Major Smith and his wife Patricia. Major Smith stood up and shook his wife's hand. Major Smith's wife, Patricia, stood up and shook her hand. When I stood up to shake LtCol Roy's wife, Diana's hand, she turned around and bent over and told me to kiss her backside. I was so shocked, when I looked at Major Smith and his wife's faces, "it was surreal". I sat down and Pam, who was at the table was another African American, shifted her body to me and whispered, "Did I just see what I saw?" Major Smith quickly asked Pam and me if we wanted tea? I said, yes. That heifer, better be happy she didn't catch me after I had a few Tequilas. All I needed was "four shots of Tequila Brave Bull" or two "Tequila, Black Russian". LtCol Roy and his wife, Diana, sat down and never looked at us. They just started talking to Major Smith and Patrice and ignored us. That Heifer showed me her backside, at a Country Club Ball, with a room full of people with lights on. "Go figure that" The former General, Payne's wife Cindy, sat directly behind me at the next table. About five minutes later, Pam said, "Let's go to the bathroom." What LtCol Roy's wife, Diana, did is called a "jackass, straight out the ghetto"." It was so embracing, that I couldn't stay at the table. Pam and I went looking for Tamar, who invited me to the Club Ball. Tamar asked Pam what happened? Tamar could see it on Pam's face, there was something wrong". I said, "I'll tell you what's wrong". **LtCol Roy's wife, Diana, told me to kiss her backside**, then unexpectedly out of Tamar's mouth she said you should have hugged her. Wow. Tamar didn't show me empathy, the next thing that came out of my mouth "was slavery" is over with". Do you know Tamar went to LtCol Roy's table shortly afterward and hugged his wife, Diana? "Sell-out" When I returned to work after the Club Ball, I told my supervisor, Mr. Carter, what LtCol Roy's wife, Diana, did to me. Mr. Carter apologizes for his supervisor's behavior. He said LtCol Roy was there for Director Connie's absences. He said Major Smith, with his quick thinking, was damage control for LtCol Roy. LtCol Roy came into my area after the Club Ball, stood on the opposite side of my desk, and said, out loud to the troops. "I am a Christian, I go to church every Sunday". He never apologizes for his wife's inappropriate behavior. How can you walk past someone and speak to them, as if nothing ever happened? When he spoke to me, I didn't speak back. I couldn't even look at him again "after his wife did to me." He was always watching me, and following me, around at all times. "Creepy right". I don't care what color you are, "right is right and wrong is wrong".

THE HEADQUARTER GRANTS 59 MINUTES

The headquarters gave 59 minutes for New Year's Eve in December 2017. Ms. Connie gave everybody 59 minutes and accepted me. She told LtCol Roy to make sure I stayed until the end of my shift, and he did. The only lights were LtCol Roy's office and the lights over my desk. It was dark, it was weird. A sensor controlled the lighting. When 4:30 p.m. came, I ran out the door. During the years, LtCol Roy and management continued not to give me the 59 minutes, and when he entered the room he would say, "Drain the swamp". LtCol Roy would tell Mr. Carter how to treat me. "Slavery is over". If he could only read my mind, "I had to play along." He came by my desk, around 2:30 p.m., and said, "Have a nice weekend", and left. All the troops were gone and my colleagues were, but he made sure he came into my area to rub it in my face. My colleague told me they got 59 minutes and asked my supervisor if I get the 59 minutes? I sent an e-mail to my supervisor asking if the 59 minutes apply to me? He came back on the email saying "not that he knows of".

CONCERNS

I had some concerns about whether I would get my promotion, security clearance, and a change in my working schedule. Director Connie set up the meeting with LtCol Roy and Mr. Carter, and it was a no-show. The first thing we talked about was my schedule. LtCol Roy launches forward in his chair, saying you're not fulfilling the one you are in. This has been going on with LtCol Roy, lying and has no evidence that I'm late. I have e-mails from 2017 to 2019 that show my time and attendance. Then we discussed my promotion. He said, "You can't get it because you don't have a security clearance". Later, I learned that the Office of Personnel Management (OPM) said I had a secret clearance, and since August 2013, an investigation was not needed. I ask him, did he hear when MSgt James Calhoun cursed at me on New Year's Eve? He said, no. I felt like I wanted to throw up. They were being dishonest. This was the plan to humiliate me. So, I ended the meeting, because I had very little tolerance for their liars. When I stepped outside the door, Ms. Connie stood outside her office and looked at me.

As soon as the meeting was over, Lt Col Roy prepared a written letter and gave it to Mr. Carter so that I could sign it. I did not sign the letter. I was on my way to the break room when I passed Lt Col Roy. "What he did next was unthinkable." As soon as I went through the double doors, where the vending machine was, I turned the corner and entered the break room. Less than a minute later, LtCol Roy passed the break room. He came through the back door of the department on the other side, which led to the break room. After he passed, I got up and stood by the vending machine, where he couldn't see me. I wanted to see "what was he up too". He tried to go to Mr. Mudd's office, but he wasn't there, so he went back to his office. "Harassment." The EEO investigator asks me if this could have been a retaliation from your previous EEO complaint? I just said, I didn't know, but it's possible. Absolutely yes, they knew that I had filed an EEO complaint at my previous job. "This is what the Hiccup is about". When an agency finds out you filed an EEO complaint, "the agency will frowned on it".

Meditation

I started praying and meditating about management, because I wanted them to leave me alone and let me do the job I was hired for. The stress had a "heavy effect on my heart". The third time I meditated, I saw Lt Col Roy in his office with a white longhorn on his right head, and then the door closed. Real time, the door was closed and he retired. "Hatred is horrific."

New Master Sergeant Kokum Wilson arrived

The new, MSgt Kokum, checked into the area to supervise the military troops, she was not friendly. When Economical Warfare Fighter Training (EWFT), held the award ceremony, I saw her and spoke to her, but she did not speak. One day, I decided to print the daily spiritual uplift, and asked MSgt Kokum if she wanted to receive them? She said, yes. You can tell that she was rude and rough, because of the way she talks to the troops. One of the phrases she says to the military troops is, "Don't make me box you in the throat". I thought it was a bit harsh in the workplace. I was told

MSgt Kokum had worked for Economical Warfare Fighter Training (EWFT), five years ago, and had inappropriate legal issues. For some reason, Tamar said, my supervisor, Mr. Carter, was involved, and that is why he had to leave before she arrived. Gary the specialist said, when MSgt Kokum was here before, she separated the military troops from the civilians. He said it took some time, after MSgt Kokum left, to get the military troops back to normal. MSgt Kokum started saying things about me, behind my back, with CW3 Peter and SSgt Carlos, who sat opposite me. She told people in the Departments that they could no longer come in her area and talk to the troops, and they would have to come through her.

Telling a Military to stop talking to me

MSgt Kokum told SSgt-Terry to stop talking to me. She constantly reminded him. She even told the troops to stop talking to me. It was clear that she didn't like me and didn't even know me. I stopped sending her the daily uplifting word because she started to acting weird.

Fixated on a sliding Door

The next thing MSgt Kokum started was fixation, on the sliding door. She asks the troops to close the door "as they come and go". She was hoping I would hop on board, and close the door behind me. "Not happening." Every time someone closes the sliding door, my desk shakes. I asked my supervisor, Mr. Mudd, why should the door be closed? "He said why not?" That was his answer. I asked Director Connie if my life is in danger, or perhaps it has something to do with MSgt Kokum? She said, no. The other departments kept their sliding door open, even sometimes when they had a quick meeting. Closing the door means you have something to hide. What happened next was surprising. As soon as it became clear what was going on behind closed doors, Ms. Connie opened the door and said, "It stays open." I would see MSgt Kokum sitting inappropriately with a few military troops, on different occasions, in the room alone. I'm also sitting in the room. I should have said, "Don't mind me, just pretend I'm not in the room."

Hostile environment, telling the Military and their family not to speak to me

By April 2018, MSgt Kokum Wilson created a hostile environment by ordering the junior military to stop talking to me. This is a poor situation, and it goes against the military's core values. As I entered the room from the back and said, "Good morning?" The troops did not speak, and they turned their back to me under the command of MSgt Kokum. They did this for three days until things returned to normal. When the military family visited their husbands, they were already given an ear full about me and how to treat me, and they did. It was their mother's children's wives, "the whole Brady Bunch." When they came into their husband's workspace, "you can see, and feel, their animosity toward me". Some of the crazy things their families have done would not look at me, if I'm not looking, they would stare at me. "Did I tell you I can be talking to you and still "see what's going on around the room?" They were staring so hard, I turned and looked at them, and they turned their heads. The whispers and the smirk on their faces. They didn't even know me, "How crazy is that?" Low self-esteem.

PROMOTING HATE

I have never seen military troops act like this, until I came to the Economic Warfare Fighter Training (EWFT). This came from the highest level to enable military troops to behave unprofessionally. "We have returned to the core values". This contradicts the core values of the Military. This went on, and nothing was ever done to these military troops. This is called promoting "hate". In September 2018, I walked in through the rear sliding door and went to my desk. MSgt Kokum was the only one in the room. I said, "Good morning," she said nothing. MSgt Kokum stopped speaking to me after two months before this happened. I smelled an odor and asked, MSgt Kokum, what is that smell? She said nothing. MSgt Kokum got up and started spraying unknown substances everywhere. I asked her why is she doing that? MSgt Kokum said, to keep the germs out. I told her I couldn't breathe with the stuff she was spraying, and I had to open the door. I opened the sliding door near my desk, and MSgt Kokum got up and closed it. I asked her why she's so disrespectful? She was so angry, until her facial expression showed she didn't care. MSgt Kokum pointed her finger at me and said, "Stop it." I told her I'd pray for her. I sat there thinking about how uncaring she was, and some of what she was doing towards me. I couldn't get back to focusing, I realized I was working in a hostile environment. I sent Mr. Mudd an e-mail telling him I was going home and why, and submitted a leave slip, and left. When I returned, I addressed what happened in detail, and sent it to Mr. Mudd and Director Connie. No response. I told them that I can't endure too much stress, that I just had a heart attack four months before I came here, and that I'm also asthmatic. They knew before I got here, I put it in an email. After the confrontation with MSgt Kokum several weeks ago, I have not been approached directly or indirectly to discuss the situation that occurred.

This procedure should have been addressed, to help eliminate further problems. In October 2018, almost a month later, management wanted to meet with MSgt Kokum, Mr. Mudd, LtCol Roy, HR, and Union representatives, and myself. Director Connie said this meeting is for me to address my "problem". If they could read my mind. I looked at the people who were going to be at the meeting, and none of them had my interest, including the Union representative from some conversations we had. I've been around many leaders; Director Connie makes it bad for other women in leadership.

All Director Connie had to do was tell MSgt Kokum to knock it off, and get back to business. But that was not in the plan. I refuse to be part of this meeting. "If you don't have common sense, don't get an education, it may not help". She sprayed some unknown substance again, this time Mr. Mudd was sitting two desks above me and the troops. I was on the phone with two customers helping me with my printer. I started choking, and I looked across, and MSgt Kokum sprayed an unknown substance toward me, smiling. The customer said you need to call us back, "when you are okay". I told the customer she was smiling, and he said she thinks it was funny, "you should call OSHA". I called OSHA and they connected me to someone to help me with MSgt Kokum, as management didn't want to do their job. They met with MSgt Kokum and Director Connie. They told them they couldn't spray in the office because some people could be allergic to the unknown substance. The email went out that no one should spray in the office.

DECLINING THE MEETING

The e-mail was sent due to negative communication, and improper work procedures within the Department. I said I am declining to move forward, with the scheduled meeting, in October 2018. Director Connie called me into her office and asked me to consider attending the meeting. The next thing she said was, "Now that we got that out the way," "Do you know she was actually, wiping off the table with her hand?" as she said this. She wanted to know "why", did you go to see the Inspector General (IG)? I asked her, how did she know? She said, your supervisor told me. I told her that I didn't feel comfortable talking about it, and I'll ask the IG if I can discuss it with you. The email I sent to General Stony about the "whistleblower" was shared with Director Connie's supervisor, that retired. I remember feeling and knowing when I looked at SES Killer's face, as I entered the building as he was leaving. I read his thoughts through his facial expression and body language. For this reason, they retaliated against me two weeks later, after sending this email to General Stony. Two of my colleagues said, "Come walk with me." Everyone knew that you sent that letter to General Stony, and what was in it.

What can we do next?

They probably said "Damn," that didn't work. The next thing MSgt Kokum did was assist Corporal Martin-Martinez in filing an Equal Employment Opportunity complaint against me. Corporal Martin Martinez ruined my name and reputation. Management supports MSgt Kokum's impulsive behavior. MSgt Kokum told the investigator she only assists Corporal Martin-Martinez, he wanted to file the complaint. Why couldn't they just come to me and ask me if I did this, before filing a complaint? No one can make me lie, or destroy the life, of another person. Especially in an African American career, we already have the hardest times.

"Black Lives Matter".

Corporal Martin-Martinez filed and EEOcompliant on me for blowing a kiss at him

When I was informed of Caporal Martin-Martinez's allegation, I was "shocked and surprised". When I first had a conversation with Corporal Martin-Martinez, he stood at his desk, with Corporal Tucker sitting on the other side of his desk. Corporal Martin-Martinez told Corporal Tucker, that he grew up poor. I asked Corporal Martin-Martinez, did he have a roof over his head and food on his table? I told him that some people have less than others. I was talking to Corporal Tucker as he stood there at his desk. Then I said, hello Corporal Tucker?, he said, "Hello Dog." I turned my head because it was shocking and disbelief, what he said. I turned around and said, "don't you ever talk to me like that again?" That kid had never disrespected me before, he was on his way out of the military.

BACK TO CORPORAL MARTIN-MARTINEZ

The next time I spoke with Corporal Martin-Martinez, it was about religion. I told him I respect everyone's religion. One day, Corporal Martin-Martinez stood in a group, with MSgt James Calhoun, Corporal Manson, and a civilian, having a conversation about religion. As he stood there, they started saying negative things about a particular "religion", so he walked away and went outside. I walked over to the group and told them Corporal Martin-Martinez was part of that religion. MSgt Calhoun said, "I don't care". MSgt Calhoun was known for that type of "mentality and attitude". When Corporal Martin-Martinez returned, I mentioned to him that I talked to MSgt Calhoun. He said he didn't care. "I care about people's feelings." When Corporal Martin-Martinez got promoted, I took pictures of him with MSgt Calhoun at the ceremony and gave them to him. I've always had the pleasure of taking pictures of people who took pictures of me when I was a model in Atlanta. I brought cake and ice cream for the troops, promoted, enlisted, left and came to the new station.

Corporal Martin-Martinez talked to me about his mother and where he was going on his vacation. One day, he came to me and said, Ms. Alexis, I met a girl who caught my attention. "I said, is she spiritual? He said, yes. I said, that's good. I gave Corporal Martin-Martinez a copy of the book "A Whisper To A Child's Ear from God". He asks me to give him another copy of the book, for his mother. I did. I have always sent an email to people who enjoyed, receiving spiritual daily uplifting. Corporal Martin-Martinez came to my desk and told me another troop wanted to receive the daily uplifting. I told him, Caporal Penny has to come and ask me herself. She has a kind spirit and has shown true leadership. Corporal Penny and SSgt Carlos always speak to me, no matter what. The problems began when the new MSgt. Kokum Wilson came on board, and wanted the sliding door closed, when you entered and out of the room. One day, I entered the rear door and said "good morning", as I passed Corporal Martin-Martinez's desk. He said, Ms. Alexis, could you come here? I walked over to his desk, and said yes? He said when you come in, can you shut the door? I was offended that he asked me to close the door, this was coming from MSgt Kokum. My voice may have gotten louder when I told him, "Absolutely Not". Then I said, "I'm not the one, meaning, don't play with me." Once, I got to my desk and sat down, "a whisper said look back". I saw MSgt Kokum run over to Corporal Martin-Martinez's desk, kneeling down and smiling with him as she asks him if he's okay. He smiled back at her, saying yes.

When MSgt Kokum is absent from work, people go and come, and the door is open at all times. When she returned, they started closing the door again. Crazy right" I felt bad that "I blew up and went off, on Corporal Martin-Martinez". I turned around and "blew him a kiss", and placed my hand on my heart. He caught the "kiss" with his fist and said, "I got it, with a smile". Corporal Tim stood next to him and looked at him when he "caught the kiss with his fist". When I had a book signing at Barnes and Noble in August 2018. I came through the front entrance and was stopped by two young ladies, Cindy and Susan. They apologized for not coming to the book signing. They yelled out, "You are a superstar", I turned to them and "blew them a kiss", and placed my hand on my heart.

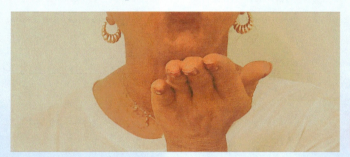 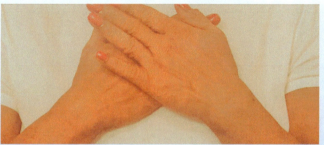

This was the process

When I was notified by the investigator, he told me who filed the EEO complaint against me. I felt in my spirit it was Corporal Martin-Martinez. I told a friend that out of all the people I knew, I thought it was Corporal Martin-Martinez the first week before I was sent home. Corporal Martin-Martinez was heavily guarded. He always had someone with him. When I would pass him, he did not speak. Corporal Martin-Martinez said I blew a kiss, and it was offensive to him. I told the investigator that when I blew the kiss at Corporal Martin-Martinez, he caught it with his fist, saying "I got it". He also smiled, and Corporal Tim was standing there when I did it. The investigator said he said I got it? I said, yes, with his fist.

He started writing and said he never mentioned that part. I remember telling the investigator that he is one of ours. **African American "sell-out".** He said, yes. Corporal Martin-Martinez was walking around with Corporal Penny and others, **"escorting him like a victim".** January 2019, I got a call from Director Connie, and her voice sounded disappointed on the phone that I was coming back. She said, "You can return to work". We met in my supervisor's Mudd's office, and she explained to me that **Corporal Martin-Martinez lied.** Now he's saying it wasn't offensive to him, lied. Director Connie couldn't let it go. She said, but that doesn't mean I tolerate that behavior in the workplace. **Then she took it a little further.** She asked Corporal Tim, who was standing next to Corporal Martin-Martinez. If I "blew him a kiss", would that be offensive to him? Corporal Tim said, yes. What choice does Corporal Tim have? He better say, yes. They are all in this together, no turning back. It's called Abuse of Authority. "She doesn't see herself". On several occasions, I have gone to Director Connie's office to talk to her. As we were having a conversation, she would start stroking my arm up and down. **"The Cat Can't Call the Kettle Black".** She was so cold to me when I returned, I had to "go back to my car and get my coat". I've never said anything bad, or had a conversation with my colleagues about Director Connie. **"Hate is a killer".** Director Connie left the room, and Mr. Mudd spoke to me afterwards. Mr. Mudd told me he had many reports for me. That's only 15% of my job, and he lied.

As Mr. Mudd walked me back to my desk, as if I had forgotten where I was sitting. He started saying, "nobody has worked on your computer". He said, "it again and again". As soon as we approached my desk, he grabbed my mouse. I remember saying, in my mind, "what the heck is going on". As soon as he touched the mouse, a name came up, and it was not my name. No big deal, it's a government computer. Every day, I dealt with the liars and manipulations. They sent me home, but Corporal Martin-Martinez was never removed, when he lied and filed a false claim to the EEO counselor against me, and was allowed to stay in the workplace. My colleagues said when I returned, management told them not to talk to me. I was isolated, and people treated me as if I were contagious or committed a crime. In their minds, they decided to hate me: "They made my life a living hell." It's mental. It has broken my heart that I was treated like this, and "my good name was tarnished." I asked the Director for a letter of apology. She gave me a letter, but no apology.

NOT FEELING AT EASE

I was not at ease, with Corporal Martin-Martinez sitting behind me. "What would they tell him to do next?" I had a nightmare, so I sent General Stony an email about my dream that frightened me. I wanted him held accountable. He said he would protect me from any reprisals. One day, Corporal Martin-Martinez stood behind me in the middle of the floor, among his MSgt Kokum, SSgt Carlos, and the other troops. "He started ranting and rating in front of them", I was extremely nervous. The next thing that came out of Corporal Martin-Martinez's mouth was shocking. He was loud, "she needs to keep her fucking mouth shut." I got up, pulled my CAC, and left.

LIKE MAYA ANGELOU SAID, WHEN THEY SHOW YOU THE REAL THEM THAT IS WHO THEY ARE

"Dreams" Spiritual guidance during my time at Economical Warfare Fighter Training (EWFT). 2016-2019

SPIRITUAL GUIDANCE

I was sitting in orientation, thinking about where I'm going to live. I was allowed to stay in temporary transit for ten days, with space available. The Union representative told me there are affordable apartments in Forest-Townhome. He showed me where they are located. The next day, I went to the apartment to check availability. I contact the landlord from the number on the building. The landlord said he didn't have any vacancies, and no further availability, as he can see. In other words, no one has given any notice to leave. I went back to the temporary transit. The clerk at the front desk said, "She can extend me for two more nights". After that, you have to check out, because we have people on orders coming in. I went back upstairs to the room, and looked at the ceiling, saying, "Lord, you brought me here". The next day, a friend called and asked me if I had the Union representative's phone number? I said, yes, let me call you back. I pulled a paper out of my purse with no name, just a phone number, and dialed it. I call the number, and a male voice answered. I said is this Mike the Union rep? He said, no. I was about to hang up, then I said I am sorry, who is this? He said it's Frank. I said, Frank, who? He said, the landlord. I said, okay. As I was about to hang up again, I said by the way? I said I know I asked you the other day, do you have any vacancies? He said, by the way, "someone is moving out as we speak, he didn't give any notice". I said, thank Jesus.

Then I need a week before I can move in. While sitting in training, I called around on base to find space available. They either had only two nights or the price was too high. I got a call from a lady from the temporary transit, she asked me how many nights I needed? I said something like four more nights. She said, "Are you sure?" Yes, ma'am, she said, "if you need more, just let me know". I cried, that was the spirit of the Lord.

A Dream

I have a friend who came with me from Accounting Lorton and Firm (ALAF). She is trying to move up in the government, and get her next promotion. She worked at Reed National Center as a GS-07. I tried to get her on, at Economical Warfare Fighter Training (EWFT). The head of the travel department told me that there would be a position opening soon. I asked Mr. Putin later, was the position announced? He said, yes, and closed. One night, I had a dream about my friend. I told my friend, I dreamt she wouldn't be working in the facility, where I worked. "It was not supposed to be". I told her, I saw her getting a promotion in travel, not here but somewhere else, and she did. Then I told her, I saw her leaving, going somewhere else, for another promotion, still in travel but at another agency. The dream came to pass. Congratulations! My friend A.N.

A Dream

I dreamed of a colleague, Mr. Den., whom I used to love, going to his office, sitting down, talking to him. One day, I told him I had a dream about him. He said what? I said no worries, it's clean, and we smiled. I told him I dreamed, that he would be leaving for a job, and not returning. I also dreamed it would be raining that day, and I would not be at work. I dreamt this dream about four months before it happened. Once I told him about the dream, he said I am leaving to go to the Pentagram temporarily, and I will be coming back. I told him I don't see him coming back. Soon it was his last day. I went into his office on a Wednesday to say goodbye. It was 80 degrees outside, with no rain. He said, actually Friday is my last day. I called in sick on Friday, unaware of that day, and didn't think anything about it. Did you know it rained on Friday, light showers? It was amazing. He never returned.

Spiritual Guidance

This person contacted me and told me her story. She said she had a colonoscopy, and they found some polyps. She said she was nervous about the test results. She said her family members died from cancer. I thought for a minute and told her I didn't see anything. Two days later, she contacted me and said the result was negative. Hallelujah!

Spiritual Guidance

One of my colleagues' family members faced medical attention. Every day for a week, I felt sick in my stomach as if something had taken over me. It would only happen around lunchtime, at my desk. I prayed, and then it stopped. The next week, on Wednesdays or Thursdays, it happened again. I prayed, and then it stopped. After about a month, my colleague returned to work. I told her that I prayed for her family member, and told her that it was as if "I felt her pain", and what she was going through. She asked me what day it was, and as she remembers, it coincides with the days I mentioned. One day, I went to the vending machine to get a snack, and my colleague's daughter was at the vending machine and said to me, are you, Alexis? She said my mother said, "You prayed for me." Then she said, "can I hug you?" It was the most amazing feeling, it touched my heart coming from a teenager. Her mother has a beautiful soul.

A DREAM

Three months before December 2019, I had a dream that I met LeBron James and his beautiful wife, Savannah. In the dream, she was smiling and so happy. She said, Alexis, let's take a picture. In the dream, Lebron was riding with the Mayor. It was a two-part dream. It switches to Christmas decorations, as if it were Christmas. "So in my mind", I thought I would see him before I retired. I'm not sure what that dream meant at that time. If I can't figure out the dream, "I put it out to the spiritual world, and wait to see what happens."

A DREAM

Another dream about LeBron James, November 2020, I prayed and meditated for three days because I was moving to another state. I said, to God, I am leaving here at the end of the month. What's going to happen? The next night, I dreamed of LeBron James wearing a white T-shirt with the biggest smile on his face. God did not allow me to see the whole dream, but I could tell it was something else there, but he shielded me from seeing it. This is my second time dreaming about LeBron James, and he is not even in my circle. "I am not a stalker".

A DREAM

Yet, another dream about Mr. James again, it was the end of April 2021.

I dreamed he was standing in our living room. Mr. James asks me, how can I help you, or what is this all about? "Something like that". In the dream, the spirit said he unexpectedly stopped by. He was in a little white vehicle, it wasn't stylish, that good way to sneak in Beaufort. In the dream, my nephew asked if he could take a picture with LeBron?.

A Dream

This happened when I lived in San Diego, California, when my family came to visit me. We planned a day at Disneyland, and I wish I had more money to splurge. During that time, I went to the military base to settle my travel orders. I got there after 2:00 p.m., and the travel officer said, anything submitted after 2:00 p.m. is processed the next day. I went home and said to myself, "I wish I had more money to splurge at Disneyland". That night when I went to bed, I dreamed $1,500.63 was deposited into my checking account. I woke up at 6:00 a.m. and called the NFCU bank. The automotive system said $1,500.63 was deposited into your checking account. "OMG, all I can say is thank you, Lord."

A Dream

This was in early 2020, when I dreamed of this dream. I dreamed that Jay-z was in a crowd surrounded by young African-American boys, and their backs were toward me. At that time, I didn't "know what the dream meant". Then I said, maybe I will be going to one of Jay-Z's concerts. I thought of this dream I had of you, Jay-z. I said, OMG, "It's the spirit of the Lord that led me to you," chosen. I researched you to get more clarity on the dream I had of you. This was now 2022. I realize God has chosen you as the voice of African Americans. It means every decision you make, say or touch in your life would be successful, according to his plan. Humbly, respectfully. I know for sure: "You have already felt this spirit of God's power." Grace has fallen on you. Mr. Carter.

Specialist Gary

When I first met IT specialist Gary, he seemed like nice person. People always give you the impression that they are a nice people, at first. "I have always said what they want". When I first arrived, I lived in temporary lodging. Once I found an apartment in Forest-Townhome, Gary offered me two chairs, because my household goods were still in storage in Florida. I asked him how much I owe him? He said nothing, someone gave it to him. Later, I decided to give him a gift card. Gary told me that his wife, Cathy, sells clothes. I started buying clothes from his wife Cathy, because I thought he could use the money. He was working two extra jobs. I started to notice that his demeanor began to change. When I asked Gary for assistance with my computer, he was always busy. I just started asking his counter partner, Paul, who sits next to him, for assistance. Have you ever asked someone to help you, and that's their job? They tell you they are busy, "but as soon as you ask someone else, they are no longer busy". One day, I talked to Paul about my son's success and dreams. Gay walked over and butted in, saying, "Your son stays in trouble". Wow, he has never met my son. I was shocked to hear that came out of his mount **Maya Angelou said, "when people show you who they are, believe them".**

I continued to talk to Paul, and ignored Gary, then he left. I have never disrespected Gary or said negative things about people in the workplace. I have always told people, "children are off-limited". When you can read people's thoughts and body language, and see people's future, "You don't have to stoop to their level".

Like "Michelle Obama said if they go low you go high". As time went on, Gary became more aggressive and hateful. One day, I told Gary that my computer was acting up, and if he gets a chance, can he look at it? He was very rude. I had two monitors and a laptop, and was only using my laptop. He asked me three times whether I wanted to use both. I keep telling him, no. The sad thing about it is that he sees the two monitors turned off, and the laptop shows me working on a program. He got mad and mumbled, under his breath, saying, "I don't have to fix your compute". "I said, whatever".

HATE LETTER ON DESK

The next thing Gary did was he placed "a hate letter on my desk". I arrived at work at 8:00 a.m. and found a hate letter sitting on my desk. I called Ann, Gary's friend from the budget department, and asked her to read it. She agreed it was a disturbing letter, and said it could be the guy who writes poems, Todd. Why would she throw Todd under the bus, for Gary? I said no, because he is not negative, and does not write these types of words. Todd writes spiritual, uplifting, and truthful poems. Ann knew, Gary placed that letter on my desk. She would rather "through Todd, under the bus" than Gary. "It's called trying to frame another brother". She left and went in the direction of Gary's office. Then, two minutes later, Gary slowly came in and walked from the opposite direction, from the rear sliding door. He asks me if I found a letter on my desk? I said, yes. He said he put it on my desk, because it contained something about dreams, so he thought it was mine. He said, he found it on top of the printer. This is what Gary meant to say. He wanted to make sure I knew it was meant for me, so he put the word "dream" in it. Then he said, "give it to me, I will place it in the wastebasket". Before Gary exited the room, he asked me, "Were you afraid?" I told him, no. I took a picture and sent it to General Stony, and nothing was done about it. I realized Gary is a coward, and I was a threat to him.

You Don't Know What You Don't Know
You Know You Don't Know
You Know You Know
You Don't Know You Know

First They Laugh At You

Then They Challenge You

Then They Admire You

Then They Use You as an Example

The dream that you don't fight for can haunt you for the rest of your life.

You never conquer the mountain, you only conquer yourself.

Talent + Luck + A = Success

A= Work Ethic

Hustle is the Variable

The Bear, The Bull, The Pig, & The Wolf... The Crows Just Watch.

I was restricted from entering the building after my regular, scheduled time. Without knowing. My work schedule is from 8:00 a.m. to 4:30 p.m. If I left and forgot something, I would be "shit" out of luck. One day, I left something on my desk and tried to re-enter, but I was unable to get back in. Captain Tony, who worked in the budget department, came in before I left. It was about 5:00 p.m. He asked me, what am I still doing here? I told him I was leaving now. I stepped out of the door into the lobby and forgot something on my desk. That is when I realized I didn't have access to get back into the office. I knocked on the door for a minute, and realized Captain Tony was not going to let me in. They sent him to see why I was still in the building. I left and never shared that information with anybody, because they already knew. I was never told, they limit my access. I only knew about it when I tried to re-enter the building or try to fax something, and it would not allow me to use my CAC. Every time I took a day off, they would go into my computer. One day, I had enough. I stood up and said out loud, "I don't mind you searching my computer, just put my files back in place." I do not have anything to hide. Director Connie instructed Gary's team to search my computer, and strict my access from using the fax machine.

GARY SET-UP TO MOVE ME

Gary was smiling at me every time I saw him. I thought about what was going on in my head. Ms. Connie told me she was moving me to Mr. Putin's department, where I was the whistleblower. The crazy thing about this is that everybody in the office knew Ms. Connie was moving me to the travel department, before I knew I was moving. Gary told me as he smiled, that I was going to move over in this travel department. I told him, I was not. Gary was hoping I would move over in that Department so badly, because they all knew I was the whistleblower who sent the email to General Stony. Penelope, that worked upstairs, said come walk with me to the store. She said everybody in the building knew about the letter you sent to General Stony. She took it a little further, and said they already gave the GS-11 to Michelle (CSR), so you will not get that promotion. General Stony let the "cat out of the bag" He told me he would protect me from reprisals. He didn't. Perhaps, I have created a scene and kept calling General Stony and sending him an email. Gary, keep telling me you are going over there. I told him I have 100% faith. He said okay, I'd be on travel and see the email traffic. At the end of the day, I went home until the investigator contacted me. **Hate can be**

deadly, "everybody was in on it, to take me down". Do you know how hard it was to pretend, and keep the pain and anger inside? **This is like a cult**

The new supervisor Mr. Mudd arrived in May 2018

When the new supervisor, Mr. Mudd, came on board, he went back and forth, passing my desk daily. A week later, he walks across from me to MSgt Kokum's desk and asks, where Alexis is? MSgt Kokum turns to me, and introduces Mr. Mudd to me. I said to him, are you my new supervisor? He walked away from me and "didn't say a word". I was the only civilian in the room who worked with the military troops. I had no problem with that. From that day forward, Mr. Mudd continues to enter the room and speak to everyone, except me. Yes, it bothered me, but what kept me going was my faith in God. When Mr. Mudd arrived, management informed him how to treat me. He walks past me, goes in and out of the building, and doesn't speak. "two wrong, don't make it right" I just stopped speaking to him also. "It feels weird".

Mr. Mudd always acts as if he couldn't hear me, a way to ignore me. Right? When someone is at my desk or on the phone, he shows up "just to see who I'm talking to". Did I tell you that" he also has selective memories? When I asked him if I could change my schedule, he ignored my e-mail. All employees at their request, in the Economical Warfare Fighter Training EWFT, are allowed to be on a flexible schedule, as they requested. I asked Mr. Mudd if I could participate in the Health and Wellness Program. He ignored my email. I sent Mr. Mudd an email asking, when will I start doing the work I was hired for? He ignored my email.

Mr. Mudd, Michelle (CSR), and management continue to weigh me down, hoping I would just leave. Michelle continues to disrespect me by sending me nasty emails. I do not reply to her emails. I brought it up to Mr. Mudd's attention. He leaned toward me as we sat at his table in his office. He pointed his finger in my face, and told me to mind my own business, and walk out. Some people would say, "if only we were outside in the parking lot."

"Like Mitchell Obama said, when they go low, you go high".

The next weird thing Mr. Mudd did was tell me the auditor wanted me to create a PowerPoint, from start to finish, on how to process an organization code. I created the PowerPoint and sent it to Mr. Mudd's email, and placed a copy on his table on the morning the auditors arrived. He never acknowledged he had received it, and never thanked me for creating the PowerPoint.

I CONTINUE TO SEND AN EMAIL TO MR. MUDD DAILY ASKING FOR WORK

I continue to send an email daily to Mr. Mudd asking him for work. He ignored me. A secret clearance is required to use the employee's name and SSN in the Accounts Process Pay System (APPS) because it's (APPS) driven. Remedy access requires a clearance to submit a remedy ticket to Accounting Lorton and Firm (ALAF) requesting special pay for employees with pay issues. Remedy a clearance, but not a secret clearance. Employees would have to provide their SSN for this system if management does not provide me with their SSN. Sometimes the employee may not be in a secured location to give you their SSN by phone, and sending an email is not an option. I asked Mr. Mudd and Michelle to provide me with the employee's SSN, but they refused. They said (AAPS) systems do not require SSN. I sent a remedy ticket to (ALAF), and they provided me with all the employee's SSNs that we pay at Economical Warfare Fighter Training (EWFT). Mr. Mudd said (AAPS) pay systems do not require SSN. "Go figure that". I sent a remedy ticket to (ALAF), and they provided me with all the employee's SSNs, that we assist in the Training Command, with pay issues. Mr. Mudd said at one point (that ALAF) probably no longer uses SSN. Ignores. Submitting a remedy ticket is about 30% of my duties. I submit a remedy ticket at least once a month, because Michelle (CSR) is not working on her reports, to ensure the employee is not on the invalid report for non-payment. Twice a month is a few too many times for an employee not to get paid. Especially if you work from home. It's unacceptable according to the agency protocol. Michelle scheduled herself to be off on payday Fridays (RDO). I remember what my first supervisor, Mr. Carter, said: "We need someone in the office for the customers when they don't get paid on payday."

I decided to File a Congressional

I requested a Congressional inquiry to be sent to Director Connie, asking her why I was not given any work, and if I will receive my promotion? Director Connie replied, "I should file a grievance if that's what I want". I told the Congressional representative, I didn't come all the way here, to be treated like this. We also talked about whether I am eligible for retirement. She said, Director Connie, said, "I was not eligible to retire". She is correct. I asked her if this will follow me. The representative said if I left and accepted another job somewhere, this Equal Employment Opportunity case could follow me. This means "it will follow me". I thought about the price I paid to relocate to Virginia and accept this job. They just "hogtie me, humiliate me, embarrass me, belittle me, and try to tarnish my good name, and tell me to hit the road jack". I don't just give up. "Slavery is over". No matter how "Dark" it gets? They are not in control, God is. I have seen Him "show up and show out". So, I will file an EEO complaint to piss them off. I told Mr. Mudd when management refused to give me work for three years and held up my security clearance for three years. It is called "Fraud, Waste, Abuse, and Obstruction of Justice".

Filing an Equal Employment Opportunity to receive work

In July 2019, Mr. Mudd called me into his office and told me that I was responsible for assuming all tasks as the CSR administrator processing pay, on the Data Personnel System Analyst Collection (DPSAC) and Accounts Process Pay System (APPS). Then he shoved the paperwork across the table to me. He seems a "little mad". This means I was just given Michelle (CSR) in Florida's work. Economical Warfare Fighter Training (EWFT), the aim is to make me fail. This order comes from the highest level. The agency frowns on you when you file an EEO complaint. I had to prepare myself for what was coming next? I knew I had to "fight and watch my back" when they gave me this work. I was set up to fail, and I was going to fight for my life, and I did.

I KNEW I HAD TO FIGHT AND WATCH MY BACK WHEN THEY GAVE ME THIS WORK.

- In July 2019, I received the new hire information that I had to enter into the "system at the end of the day". The (CSR) Michelle should have entered the new hire information into the system the week before she handed it to me.

- In August 2019, I input the employee work schedule as Maxi/flex. My supervisor, Mr. Mudd, came to my desk and sat down, and told me to change the employee's work schedule to (C21-6). I had previously sent Mr. Mudd an email telling him that some of these employees' work schedules were obsolete. In some cases, I had to track down the employees, letting them know they needed to fill out another work schedule. The next day, I viewed the pay detail, and it showed the employee, Mr. Mudd, told me to change his schedule to (C21-6), wasn't going to get paid. On the morning of pay detail, I changed that employee's work schedule back to the Maxi/flex schedule to (99-5) to ensure he gets paid. I said I would work on his schedule after payday. Before the system went down, on that same day, Mr. Mudd went behind my back and had Michelle change the employee's work schedule back to schedule (C21-6) without informing me. Michelle changed the schedule in the Data Personnel System Analyst Collection (DPSAC). She failed to change it in the Accounts Process Pay System (APPS). A last-minute schedule change would have to be changed in (APPS), because it would be too late to flow through the system. Mr. Mudd said it was my fault that the employee didn't get a paycheck, and Director Connie echoed behind him. I showed Mr. Mudd the audit report, which showed Michelle was the last person to make changes to the employee record. Mr. Mudd and Director Connie still said it was my fault. They didn't count on me knowing how to find the audit report in the Data Personnel System Analyst Collection (DPSAC). God sent me an angel from the Pentagram who walked me through where to find this information in the Data Personnel System Analyst Collection (DPSAC). I had just started learning that system hands-on.

- I asked Mr. Mudd for the Human Resources contact email, he said no. On one occasion, I had to contact the employee about receiving his schedule. The employee said he never accepted the position. I ask Mr. Mudd again for HR contact information to notify the employee who accepted the position. Once I contact the HR specialist, she apologizes for not sending the information beforehand. These "documents" are filled out, and accepted by four different people, before I receive them. Michelle, and Mr. Mudd, are the last two people before I receive the documents. Michelle incorrectly sends the forms to the supervisor. Michelle could make sure the employee's paperwork of his/her schedules is corrected, since she doesn't have anything else to do.

- Mr. Mudd said the employees were calling and asking about not being able to log in to the Data Personnel System Analyst Collection (DPSAC) to post their timecards. I ask him to send me the names of all the employees who have problems logging in. He sent me one employee's name. I thought he said, many employees. Mr. Mudd asks to see the employee's work schedule that just check-in. He said this work schedule is incorrect. I told him, this is what you and Michelle always sent me. He said he can't tell who is the employee supervisor, by the signature. Mr. Mudd said, "Do you know this employee, Richard, is a GS-14?" I said, yes. I said to myself, "what grade got to do with a schedule". Mr. Mudd has been sending me other employees' work schedules, not signed by their supervisor. He told me to contact Richard and tell him, if he doesn't fill out another work schedule form, he won't get paid. I didn't tell Richard that, because my goal has always been to ensure the employee gets paid, "no matter what". When Mr. Mudd said, GS-14 would not be paid. I said, "Maybe Mr. Mudd and Richard know each other, and I'm it". It was obvious, from the time Richard entered the door to check-in, and asked to use my desk phone, with his mobile phone in his hand. The call Richard made sounded like he was confirming a package, "everything okay here". Nice guys, he sat down with me and chilled for a minute.

- An employee contacted me, saying she didn't receive her paycheck. I looked at her records in both systems to see why she didn't get paid. I told her that I sent an email to your supervisor telling him he needed to correct your timecard. I also told him that she showed up on the report, as "regular 8 hours should have not been reported", he never responded. This employee went on active-duty reserve. When she returned, HR did not return her to duty (292), so she didn't get paid. When an employee returns to duty, he must notify his/her supervisor, and then the supervisor informs the HR/personnel to process the return to duty. When it showed up on the report, it was too late for personnel to process it promptly for the employee to get paid. "Here we go again". Mr. Mudd and Director Connie blamed me for why the employee

didn't get paid. Ms. Connie told Mr. Mudd to contact the employee's A/O and to send her the email. She is talking about when I told the A / O earlier, that the employee was on the report. Ms. Connie asked me to explain what happened? I sent Ms. Connie the remedy ticket from Accounting Lorton and Firm (ALAF) so they can explain it to Mr. Mudd and Ms. Connie in "English", because they are not comprehending it. Mr. Mudd and Ms. Connie told the employee supervisor it was my fault. I had to deal with this every day.
"Hatred is Horrific".

- In the first week, the customer was told to contact me to see if he would get paid, and "don't trust me". One guy was a "bit scary", and I've never seen him before. He tried to use "an intimidation tactic on me". He came to my desk and "stood close up on me" and asked me if he was going to get paid, and how could he trust me? People were coming from upstairs and calling, asking me if they were going to get paid. A supervisor called and said, his employees asked if I'm the CSR or the other Michelle, is the CSR? I said I'm the CSR. When I went over to talk to the Inspector-General (IG), he said he would see my name, Alexis, one week, and the next week, he would see Michelle's name, on the broadcasting bulletin. Between all this chaos, I manage to make sure everybody gets paid. I printed out everything I processed and then locked it in a drawer. Later, I realize they have a key to my drawer. That old saying, "You can run, but you can't hide".

- When I asked Mr. Mudd, why do MSgt Kokum want to keep the door closed? He said, why not? He said, "You don't know what MSgt Kokum has to do to get the military troops ready". He said, "You would have to be a military troop to understand." What an ignorant statement! All my life, that's all I knew, and I was married to a military member. Go-figure that.

- One day, Mr. Mudd came to my desk and sat down, and started talking to me about Accounting Lorton and Firm (ALAF), and what the auditor expects, going forward. He started asking me "some stupid questions." He asks me in front of the troops to belittle me. He asked me, "What does "LS mean?" Then he said, "What does LA mean?" Then he asks me how many codes does (ALAF) have in its system? I told him that it's not required to know how many codes, it's irrelevant. I had an (APPS), manual processing pay book on my desk. He asks me, "How old is this book?" Then said (ALAF), probably does not use SSN anymore. Mr. Mudd was still trying to humiliate me, in front of all the troops, in the room. Everybody was quiet in the room, you can hear a pin drop.

This was not the first time and would not be the last. One day, he caught me off guard. Mr. Mudd has been coming into the room with no respect, "telling me, not asking me" to log in to the (APPS) system. I said for what? He said, "Just log in". I said, no. He said I was insubordination, and "he could fire me if I didn't do what he said". I jumped up and said "fire me" and took a walk outside. "I had enough". Later, when I returned to my desk, he asked me again. I said no, and leave me alone, and you are stressing me out. I ignored him. Before the end of the week, he wrote me up. I signed it, and below the line I said, I don't agree. Then later I added to the letter: When I asked you to give me work, you ignored me. That's called Fraud, Waste, and Abuse. I should have called them, but I didn't.

COUNTING DOWN

He asked me why, didn't I notify him when the employee was on the uncertified report? I said, what do you mean? I told him, I send you the reports, after working it as scheduled, and before and after pay goes down. He asks me what will you do about the supervisors, who are not certifying their employees' timecards in a timely matter. I told him I am working on making some changes. I cannot make the supervisor certify their employee's timecard. All I can do is continue emailing and calling the supervisors, telling them to certify their employee's timecards. I told him "it is his responsibility" to ensure that supervisors do not continue to take it for granted, by not certifying their employees' timecards. I told Mr. Mudd he needs to sit down with the supervisor first, and if they do not comply, take it up the change of command. He tries to make it look as if it's my responsibility. Michelle has always had the same problems, with the supervisor not certifying the employee's timecard, before I arrived. The next question he asked was, why am I processing SF1150? . I told him, if the employee comes from a non-DOD agency, I send the SF1150 to Accounting Lorton and Firm (ALAF). If it's a delay and it's too late to send it to the Accounts Process Pay System (APPS), I will input the employee's leave balance to their account.

Once Mr. Mudd was finished going over my progress review, he told me to go to my desk and sign off on it. Then he said, wait a minute, he handed me a paper on a word document, before walking out. He wrote me up and said all the customers were complaining, and your work was unsatisfactory, and the customers could not comprehend what I was saying. Mr. Mudd said, "This is just a progress review," don't worry. I went to my desk, and as soon as I sat down, he summited me back in his office. Mr. Mudd was sitting with DiVall, from upstairs. I had just told Sharon three weeks ago to watch out for her. I also told Sharon, that Cruella Devil made, my stomach hurt. "That was the spirit". Mr. Mudd said this is a Performance Improvement Plan (PIP). As soon as he said that, I went off on Mr. Mudd and Cruella Devil, and pointed my finger at them, and told them, I came here to work, and "this is how I am treated". "I had enough". I stayed home for two days sick, to my stomach, trying to figure out what I should do. "If I don't leave, they will fire me".

Meditation

I also meditated about Mr. Mudd around the same time as I meditated about Director Connie and LtCol Roy. I wanted Mr. Mudd to leave, because he was breaking my heart. As I saw the others in the meditation, it revealed Mr. Mudd leaving. I saw Mr. Mudd and Mr. Putin leaving simultaneously.

Asking God what should I do?

I ask God, what am I going to do now? He said, "Let me take you down memory lane". I have prepared you for this day. When you filed a Congressional, I had the lady casually talk to you about retirement. Remember she asked you if you could retire? That was Me, your Heavenly Father. Then God said I sent you a figure of yourself sitting in front of you. It was a quick reflection of you. It said, retire. Yes, I remember that. Then God said, "Do you remember when you first arrived here in 2016, you asked me if this is your last assignment?" I answered you, I said, yes. It is time to go, on your next assignment, your journey is not over. I felt so relieved after the spirit of the Lord spoke to me. It looks dark on the outside, but when you look through me and God's eyes, it is full of light that makes me keep going. I see everything with His power. It's called Faith.

The second day, I sent an email to General Stony telling him, I am at the point that I am almost having a nervous breakdown. It's been hell. I came to Economical Warfare Fighter Training (EWFT) to work. On Friday, November 2019, I realized this situation has gotten worse. I was now being placed on a performance improvement plan (PIP). I knew it was time for me to go. All my life people have been trying to take advantage of me, but when I stand against them, I become the problem. I told General Stony that I would retire. He said Alexis, did you let your supervisor know? I said yes, I sent Mr. Mudd an email telling him, I was retiring.

THE DAY I MEET GENERAL ROBERT STONY

Before I get started, I would like to ask anyone, **"have they ever been hypnotized?"** Okay, "this is weird, I think I was". As I returned from a doctor's appointment, as I "walked up the ramp going into the door of the lobby of my job". I remember a hand, in a color of military uniform, holding the door for me. After that, I didn't remember standing in the lobby or going to the next door, swiping my CAC,

to enter the office door. It was almost as if this person was waiting for me in the lobby, returning from my doctor's appointment. It was the strangest thing, I didn't remember standing in the lobby. I remember everything, because I'm gifted.

NEXT

I was sitting at my desk, taking a training course, when Director Connie came in and stood behind my chair, with her back to me. I didn't turn around, because she stood behind my chair so close, and introduced MSgt Kokum to someone. Director Connie talked about MSgt Kokum like, she was "someone important". Ms. Connie continues to go on at this point. "It was rude, disrespectful, and unprofessional" for her to stand behind my chair having a conversation. I can feel her vibration close behind me. It was annoying, in my ear, so I turned around. As I turned around in my chair, I was "facing five people in the room". Soon as I turned around, General Stony "grabs my hand, shakes it, and walks off like a duck". That was weird. General Stony never introduced himself. (Red flag) I found out later, that the people in the room were General Stony, and his assistant, LtCol Roy, Director Connie, and MSgt Kokum Wilson.

When I worked for (ALAF), when a high-ranking General or SES is visiting, it's announced the time he/she will arrive, so everybody can be at their desk. That was the protocol throughout my career. The room was empty, and the military troops were out or at lunch that day. Then the General or SES will be announced again on board, and you stand at attention at your desk or if it's going to be held in the auditorium, we stand. That was how it was done throughout my career. The room was empty, and the military was not around that day. Unprofessional. "Go figure that".

NEXT-CINDY (REFERENCE NAME TO THE GROUP LIST)

Cindy asked me a few times did I want to attend the General luncheon? I decide to attend. This meeting was supposed to address the problems of Economical Warfare Fighter Training (EWFT), which is taking place in the workplace. She told me that people "complained to EEO about the agency, and they were unhappy". Cindy said, General Stony was sent here, but did not want to come. We all had the opportunity to address our issues. Most of the people who attended the luncheon worked for General Stony. They went around the table and introduced themselves. Then the floor was open to anyone with questions. I asked a question and had a moment when I couldn't think of what I wanted to say. Susan stepped in and said, what she thought, I wanted to say. "It took her a minute to get there", I said, okay, whatever. I wanted to address something more privately, so I asked General Stony, do he have a suggestion box? He said, what is that? I said it's a box placed somewhere by your office door that anyone can put their questions or concerns in the box, and it can be addressed, "without anyone knowing who said it". He said, "Are you scared?" I said, no. General Stony said, then send me an email. I said, okay. I'm not afraid of anyone other than my heavenly father, as long as I'm pleasing Him. Before going to General Stony luncheon, Mr. Mudd said when you come back, I want to know what the meeting was about. I said, okay. When I returned, I told Mr. Mudd exactly what I said. The people at the meeting had already told management what I had said. Cindy started calling me, saying General Stony is still waiting on your email, and said, he might start walking around. I did not immediately send the email to General Stony. Cindy calls again to enforce what General Stony continues to say: "He is still waiting."

General Robert Stony said he will, protect me from any reprisal

I received an email from the Inspector General (IG) asking to meet with him. I said yes. I sent Mr. Mudd an email request to talk to the Inspector General (IG), and he said yes. I spoke to the IG about the whistleblower letter I sent, General Stony.

Inspector General (IG) Guy

Guy asked me with a smile, which one do you rather have first, the promotion, or security clearance? said my security clearance first. He wrote it down and said, he will check on it immediately. I spoke to my girlfriend, who worked in the IG office at headquarters. She said I should have gone online, and contacted the independent Inspector General (IG). Because "You will get nowhere". After all, they are in with the agency. I know Guy (IG), never investigated my security clearance. If he had done it, I would have received it. The order is coming from General Stony. Remember, the Office of Personnel (OPM) said I didn't need a background check. I already had a level of secrets clearance before I came on board.

The Inspector General, Guy told me to contact the OSC

The Inspector General, Guy, said, "If you believe you have been retaliated against", your proper recourse as a civilian is to contact - The Office of Special Counsel (OSC): I did contact the OSC and put in my complaint, and was told by Lisa I did not have any basis. I could have appealed, but look at where we are today.

Abuse of Authority

www.osc.gov
Whistleblower Disclosure Hotline
1730 M Street, N.W., Suite 21B
Washington, D.C. 20036-4505

ADMITTING IT WAS WRONG AND TO MAKE IT RIGHT

One of the young ladies, I mentioned in the whistleblower letter, was fired by her supervisor, Mr. Putin. When Gloria returned to work, she received a contract job for four months and was back on the street trying to feed her family. I met a young lady named Emily, who worked seven years ago for Economical Warfare Fighter Training (EWFT) when she was a GS-07. She visited some friends who still worked in the budget department. She asked if Mr. Putin was here in the office? He was. She said, when she worked under him in the travel department, he humiliated her and belittled her in front of her colleagues. Emily said when she used the phone, he yelled at her. She said, she still gets emotional when she sees him. There are many other victims of Mr. Putin's abuse. I remember an African American who just arrived that week. He yelled at her, but she fought back. She told Mr. Putin you will not disrespect me. I asked one of the colleagues who worked for him why he shouts and curses his employees? He said this is "nothing to compare with what he used to be". He said management has never done anything. I heard him go off, "on some trivial things", and "it doesn't take much". It irritates me, I just can't stand by and hear Mr. Putin humiliate and disrespect his employees. For this reason, I sent General Stony a whistleblower letter.

LOCAL SECURITY KEPT ME IN THE LOOP ABOUT MY SECURITY CLEARANCE

The local security Barbara continues to ask the Office of Personnel Management (OPM) for the status of my security clearance over the past years. OPM kept telling Barbara they were closing my case, but never did. Does Director Connie have the authority, "rather you get your security clearance," even if you already have clearance from the previous agency? I was standing in the doorway of Director Connie's office when she asked me if I received my security clearance? I said, no. She replied, "I will check on it". "What kind of question is that?" she knows. When she asked me, "she was rubbing my right arm up and down." Barbara said she doesn't know why they wouldn't close your case, because you didn't need a background check. Director Connie never got back to me about clearance. Office of Personnel Management (OPM), said they didn't have to investigate Alexis, because she already had a secret clearance from her previous jobs. In May 2017, an investigator came to my house to identify me and verify that I lived at that address. My background check was completed shortly afterward. Director Connie "knew I was the whistleblower". She wanted to set an example for those who go against the agency, by filing an EEO complaint. Once I was sent home on administrative leave, General Stony sent me an email. He said he looked at the case, and that we needed to take a step back, and let it process. Abuse of Authority. Once I returned from administrative leave, I still did not have my security clearance. I sent General Stony an email telling him I still don't have my security clearance, and "I guess I will be going to counseling". The next day, I received my security clearance. "Can you believe this crap?" Go figure that. General Stony knew everything that was going on with me, and how they were treating me. They acted on his order: "Torture me, humiliate me, embarrassed me," and did nothing. Economical Warfare Fighter Training (EWFT), informed General Stony of my previous EEO complaint.

General Stony told me, "at one point, to stop emailing him" and follow the chain of command. I told him, "They are the problem." I would still send him an e-mail, "it is about accountability". General Stony said: "He will protect me from reprisals." He doesn't get to quit. They were always talking smack and laughing behind my back. I decide to print out General Stony's picture, and place it on my wall, "to get a reaction and a good conversation going". People would stop and ask me why "Do I have General Stony's picture hung up on my wall at my desk?" I would say just because, or give a different answer, every time they ask me.

BACKGROUND INVESTIGATION

Once you have accepted a position in the Federal Government, the investigation begins with your background check. The scope of the background investigation depends on the clearance required by the agency. Since I have been in the federal government for over 20 years, my background check would be routine, but not limited, as long as I have not violated the law of the federal government. Once your background check is complete, the agency's director determines whether she has approval or disapproval of the outcome of the investigation. The Office of Personnel Management National Background Investigation Service "My Case Closed Dated August 11, 2013" The transmittal I received shows no background investigation was **completed on Aug 11, 2013.** I already had a secret clearance. Secret Clearance lasts ten years.

DISCRIMINATION

Economical Warfare Fighter Training (EWFT), has violence, my Constitution Rights. Discrimination against me". "Abuse of authority" denied me work. Fraud, Waste and Abuse. False allegation charges against me. "Held up my secret clearance".

Title VII of the Civil Rights Act of 1964. Title VII prohibits employment discrimination based on race, color, religion, sex and national origin.

The new LtCol Jeff Macintosh We'll just call him "Uncle

When the new LtCol Jeff Macintosh arrived, he went around introducing himself.

It is an advantage for me when people think I'm naïve. "I am just polite".

I saw LtCol Jeff Macintosh coming up behind me, after talking to the military troops. He started walking out the door and came back and said, who are you? I told him my name is Alexis, and he shook my hand. "Here we go again, pretending". Sometimes I want to say something, but the spirit says, no, no, Alexis, do not say anything. Okay. LtCol Macintosh was already informed of the Equal Employment Opportunity (EEO) complaint I filed at my previous job, and on Economical, Warfare Fighter Training (EWFT) for not giving me work. He never introduced himself, as the new Lieutenant Colonel. Then someone came to my desk to check in. When I saw LtCol Macintosh go into the office of the old LtCol Roy's office, that's when I said, "Oh, that's the new LtCol." This was after I told General Stony and Mr. Mudd I was retiring, when I met LtCol Macintosh. One day, LtCol Macintosh called me into his office to talk to him. He said people "were saying negative things about you", so he decided he wanted to hear what I had to say. He asked me if I would consider staying? I said no. Then he said he wishes he was here earlier, "thinking in mine, so he can harass me too". He asked me what happened? I started to tell him what happened, and he launched forward to me in his chair, and said, "Don't you say anything negative?" (Red flag).

"Remember, this is like a cult". I felt like I was on the edge of a cliff-hanging every day. I started talking about the CSR, Michelle in Florida, "he said I do not want to talk about her". I told him I wasn't given any work to do. "quiet, did not have any comment". Then he asked me if I would consider, "Michelle to be your supervisor?" Now we're talking, "True color just came out" Here we go, it didn't take long.

Michelle was one of the few I filed an EEO complaint against. He knew it. "Hatred is Horrific". This guy did not even know me. "Ignorant". I was trying to be polite, I said, no. I told him I'm going to meet Oprah one day. He launched forward in his chair, and said, "I do not doubt it", and said, "Tell Oprah hello for me". "Sarcastic and arrogant". LtCol Macintosh said, "I am worried about you, are you able to retire?" I said yes. Then he asked me, what I wanted for my retirement? I said nothing. He kept insisting he do something for me, I said, no. He made a joke about General Stony and their friendship. "He was the only one smiling". Then he said, "Did they place you on a Performance Improvement Plan (PIP) with no warning?" I said yes. "He acts so surprisingly". I told LtCol Macintosh that I told management I had a heart attack three months before coming here. He said you did? "He was so comical". When I returned after the heart attack in December 2019, LtCol Macintosh insisted on reading a farewell note to me in Mr. Mudd's office. "It was like talking to a child". After I had told him twice, I did not want him to give a speech. He still insists on giving the farewell speech on purpose. "Harassment".

I just wanted my retirement package and leave. I had just gotten out of the hospital and was very weak. He went against what I had asked him not to do. "No, respect, heartless". No empathy towards women. "I know the kind, yes the kind" He called me in his office on my last day, before he read my goodbye, and said he was praying I would not die. What he was hoping for, "if I die, the EEO case would magically disappear". "Did I tell you he is the Budget Officer? "Go figure that". As he started reading my farewell letter, he said "Director Connie said she wishes she could be here". "He repeated it over, and over, repeatedly as he read". Then he talks about keeping my head up, 'like I have low self-esteem". Sometimes people "do not see themselves" and don't realize they've lost their way. God shielded me from "low self-esteem", so I could go about His business. He didn't want me distracted. Mr. Mudd started looking at LtCol Macintosh as he kept going on about nothing. I could not wait to run out of there. "I am just polite". Economical Warfare Fighter Training had already "beaten me down for three years". But LtCol Jeff had to deliver the last blow for General Stony. I would say he's an "Uncle Tom", I always tell people "slavery is over" if you didn't know". **Deuce**

THESE ARE NAMES THAT HAS BEEN CHANGED

SHARON, CINDY, SUSAN, TERRY, BERRY, CRUELLA DEVIL AND TAMAR

I am friends with everybody, it's not unusual. Everyone is my friend who wants to be my friend. The connection is the spirit of the Lord. I have friends I had conversations with on the phone, and we exchanged gifts, and I never met them.

SHARON

When I first met Sharon, she checked in to Economical Warfare Fighter Training (EWFT), she was friendly. I would see her in a few of my training classes, and then when I attended General Stony's luncheon. One day, Sharon came downstairs to my desk and sat down to talk to me. The first thing, she said, I don't care for the MSgt Kokum Wilson, sitting across from you. (Red flag). I didn't say anything, "because I saw where it was going". The next time Sharon came downstairs, she told me I needed to be careful with Cindy. She said Cindy visits General Stony's office every morning at 10:00 a.m. When I didn't respond to her statement the next time, she made sure she reiterated to me about trusting Cindy. Sharon said one morning she went with Cindy to see General Stony. I said, okay thanks. (Red flag). Sharon called me, and asked me to come, and meet her in the restroom. She had some concerns about testifying in a case where she had made a statement of what she knew about an employee at a previous agency. I told Sharon if she doesn't want to give her opinion, just tell them that. "That's your right". After Sharon went back upstairs, I was not satisfied with the advice I gave her. I immediately sent her an email telling her to follow, "her heart and what, Jesus would have wanted, her to do". I did get advice from Sharon when someone placed a hate letter on my desk. She read it, and "googled it to see if it was a song", and it was not". I sent it to General Stony. The next time I saw her, she told me that Terry, who I introduced Sharon to, said something inappropriate to her. She said he placed his hand on her shoulder and told her: "He was once lost, and she has to pray for forgiveness". (Red flag). It's amazing how their relationship developed so quickly. She said she wanted to curse him out, but she ran to her car and prayed. "They both tried to figure out what each other was," at least that's what she was saying. She asked me, "doesn't Terry look like he could be?" I told Sharon, I didn't look at Terry like that. She said, "You're good, I didn't know what the heck she meant".

Before I left her desk, I asked Sharon about lunch with Cindy? She made sure I knew she wasn't interested in having lunch with Cindy. The next time I saw Sharon, she said Cindy went off on her. "Here we go again, with all that drama". She said Cindy told the people upstairs she couldn't work in this condition. Then Sharon showed me a paper document that she kept notes on, how Cindy was talking to her. I read it and said, "You are doing the right thing if that's how you feel". Sharon told me Cindy filed an Equal Employment Opportunity Complaint against her supervisor. "Who cares" She said Cindy requested to move out of that area, and the request was not granted. Instead, they "built a wall as high as the TV mount". Cindy's complaint was too much noise, and the stuff on the television was inappropriate in the workplace. "I remember catching Cindy twice at Sharon's desk", they didn't know that I had seen them, before they saw me. "Cindy walked away quickly, they look ridiculous". "Remember, they allegedly don't like each other". Cindy had **stopped, speaking to me** for some time. Sharon, yet again drama, told me some stuff about Cindy. After Sharon left and went back upstairs, I quickly emailed Sharon about Cindy. I said Cindy never did anything to me, other than being nice to me. I knew Sharon was going somewhere with that drama, that's why I sent the email. **"It's called set a bait".** The next day, I passed Cindy when she was in the elevator going up. Cindy was smiling, and said "Hello" and wanted me to take the elevator with her. "I said, Holy Jesus". **Sharon took the bait** and shared the email with Cindy. Remember, Cindy stopped talking to me. "Go figure that".

Sharon came back downstairs and told me that two of my colleagues were upstairs talking to Cindy. "Who cares". She asks me why are they there? I told Sharon, maybe Cindy called her friends for support. That's what those girls in the budget department do, check on you. She said she didn't like one of them. I think the reader can figure out which "one". Go-figure that. The next time Sharon came downstairs, she told me about a conversation she had with Cindy at her desk disrespecting her. Sharon said Cindy was "talking down to her", and the employee on the other side of the cubicle overheard and told her supervisor, Cruella Devil. Cruella Devil told Sharon's supervisor, Ms. Green, about Sharon and Cindy's conversation. When Sharon told me what Cruell Devil said, I started getting sick to my stomach. "The spirit told me that this conversation was based on lies". "This is some junior high school stuff, no elementary stuff, OMG. It made me nauseous". When I returned from the break room, I felt sick. When I left for the day, I told Sharon to come into the lobby and meet me outside. I told Sharon the spirit reveals, that Cruella Devil "is a negative dark spirit, and I can't be part of this". I told her I didn't want to hear anything, more about their conversation. She ignored me, and walked away as she "yelled" to a friend in the parking lot. She didn't even say excuse me, and we never spoke again. I'm just polite. The next thing that happens weeks ahead. I was placed on a performance improvement plan (PIP). Guess who was in the room assisting him? Cruella Devil. "BINGO"

Cindy

When I first met Cindy, part of her job was to collect information for the newspaper. When I had the book signing at B & N in August 2018, she asked, can she put what I accomplished in the newspaper? I said, yes. Her other tasks were to get as many people as possible to join the Sergeant Major Whitfield, for a cup of coffee, and the General Stony for lunch. I attended the luncheon among others, Sharon, Cindy, Susan, and Berry sitting next to General Stony. First, we went around the table, introducing ourselves. Then they opened the floor for anyone who wanted to ask a question. When it was my turn, I asked General Stony if he had a suggested box, so you can drop a note anonymously addressed to him. He said, no. I wanted to send something privately to him. General Stony asks me if I am scared? I said, no. General Stony said to send him an email. Everybody in the room heard when General Stony said to send him the email. I did not send General Stony the email immediately. Cindy called me and told me that General Stony is still waiting for the email. Cindy said General Stony is talking about coming over, and walking around in the building. Cindy was always calling me and acting like, "I'm asking her for advice". One day, Cindy called me and told me that General Stony embarrassed her, in front of all the guests in the room. I told her to get on his calendar and asked for a meeting with General Stony. She said she tried to, but he appointed someone in his administration to talk to her. Every time I met with her, she always has something to say about General Stony. "I was a good listener". Cindy also played the role Susan was after her job. She always asks for my input. She said, "What do you think?" I told her "yes I think she after your job". She looked surprised. I liked where she was going with this.

One of the crazy thing about her. She would always ask me if she looks good? Then she would say, "I know I look good". It was strange, and I didn't feel comfortable having these conversations. Cindy had a smart mouth and was immature. I didn't have much empathy for her. It ate at the core of me, when she tried, to give me advice. I'm just polite. Many times Cindy called me at home, and tried to get information from me, and then one day, "I snapped". She said, "Let me let you go". I said, okay. I have very little tolerance for drama. I told her that General Stony told me to "stopped sending him e-mails", and go through "the chain of command". I reply to General Stony, that "they are the problem". I didn't tell Cindy what my reply was to General Stony.

One day, I just came out and told her that General Stony told me to "stop emailing him". "It was like I just opened up a can of worms". Every time she saw me, the question came up. "How did you feel when General Stony told you to stop e-mailing him?" This is what I kept telling her. "General Stony can only do so much". She asked the same question every time she saw me. "She caught me off guard, I may have snapped". For this reason, she stopped talking to me. "She acts as if I were in counseling". I was glad "she was weighing me down". I'm just polite.

Susan

During a fire drill, I met Susan in the hallway. Susan told me when I got a chance, come over and meet her son. Susan induces me to her husband and son. I join them on the dance floor of the Ball. That was the start of our friendship. I introduced Susan to my son, when he came to pick me up, from work. I would go upstairs from time to time and have a conversation with Susan. She mainly talked about her children and colleagues who don't like or talk to her. One day, I was leaving to go back downstairs. Susan told Ms. Connie that she was still looking forward to her "being her mentor". I thought what she was doing was unprofessional. But there is a motive behind it, "to initiate a chain reaction". I looked at Susan and said, "See you later". I thought about what she said, dismissed it, and decided to give her another shot. (Red Flag). Susan asks me, on several occasions, again. I never told Ms. Connie what Susan said. I just felt it was a personal thing, and it was strange. At the General Stony luncheon, Susan spoke up for me, what she thought I was trying to say. I had a question, but was not able to express myself what I wanted to say. It took her a minute, but eventually, she landed the plane. When I returned from administrative leave, it was Sharon, Cindy, and Susan who joined me in the lobby, with a welcome back gift and signed card. I remember saying how nice and caring they were. After talking with me for a minute, Sharon and Cindy head back upstairs. Susan stayed, and what she said was "shocking". She told me to "get my resume together and leave". Just like that. Can you believe that "heifer?". How sad, she asked me to send her and her friend the daily, spiritual uplift every day. I didn't see this coming, she's part of something negative. Susan said, "I just think you should leave". Who put that heifer in charge? "God, can you come down here and tell these folks who we are?" I remember noticing her facial expression was so "dark". The next time I saw her, we all headed to a mandatory meeting across the street. Susan saw me coming into the lobby and looked away. Director Connie was in front of me. Susan spoke to Director Connie and kept on trucking. I wasn't surprised she didn't speak. One day, Susan sent me an email saying she had been thinking about me. What a joke. I deleted the email". I'm just polite. The last time I saw her leaving the building, "Susan spoke to me, I spoke to her". Hatred is Horrific.

TERRY

When I met Terry for the first time, he came to my desk and said he was sexually abused. He left, came back, and started showing me the text from the person. I told Terry, I'll pray for him, I didn't even know him. He just stopped, at my desk, and told me his story. The next week Terry came into the area and told the "troops behind me out loud that he was sexually abused." "He told the troops that he was not ashamed of saying it". MSgt Kokum asked him to leave, because she didn't like his tone. When Terry came back, he started spiritually talking to the troops. Terry asked me to come to his office, and listen to some spiritual music. It was enjoyable. Sometimes I shared my music with Terry. I have always sent one or two lines of spiritual uplifting every day, no matter where you are in the world. Terry was always "imitating Tyler Perry", and he was good at it. "He knew all Tyler Perry lines by memory". I always enjoy listening to him. I would always tell him "do it again". I decided to send Terry's name to an audition, when Mr. Perry was looking for people for an up-and-coming film in Alexandria. The craziest thing was when he had the chance to audition, he didn't go. One day, out of the blue, he said MSgt Kokum did not want me to talk to you. I said, okay. Remember, "there is a motive behind this, to trigger a chain reaction". I would not go to his office for a while, until he called me, to listen to his song. (Red Flag). Over time, Terry reminded me that MSgt Kokum kept asking him, "Why are you still talking to her?" MSgt Kokum said, "didn't I tell you about talking to her?" It was strange because he did not fall under MSgt Kokum Wilson. I told Terry she didn't tell her SSgt Carlos not to speak to me. SSgt Carlos speaks to me in front of her, and when she is not around. I told Terry, that MSgt Kokum should not control who you are talking to. If he could only read, my mind. One day, "he finally showed his true color". Terry said, "Did I tell you I voted for the current president?" This was in 2019 when he said this. I said you have the right to vote, for whoever you want to be president. I told Terry she doesn't tell her SSgt Carlos not to speak to me. SSgt Carlos speaks to me in front of her and when she is not around. Months later, it came up again. Terry was in the back area where the vending machine was. I went back there to get a snack, and Terry said it again. "Did I tell you that I voted for the current president?" I said, yes, and you already told me that. Then, what he said next caught me off guard. Terry said, "You know why I voted for the current President because formal President Obama didn't do anything for us". I said, okay. Then he said the word "Hate". Terry said **"he hated President Obama",** and he said it more than once. Then he said again, **"with anger and rage".** "Now he pissed me off, **I snapped".** I backed him up into the vending machine without touching him, pointing my two figures toward him, and said how can you hate someone you never met? How can you **call yourself a Christian,** and say you "hate Obama?" I caught myself and backed off. He ran to his office. I went behind him, and said, "Hey," but he didn't turn around. He kept his back toward me. I stayed friends with him because Terry was so messed up, and very emotional at times.

Terry had some good qualities, especially when I asked him for a ride home. "Go figure that". Smile. One day, Cindy said to me, that Terry is a very emotional person. I said, yes. How did she know this, and shared it with me? Wow, busy. Remember, it's like a cult, they have to stick together. Terry took me to lunch once, just to get information out of me, I think. When he left to go to his next duty station, he didn't even say goodbye. "Hatred is Horrific"

BERRY

MSgt Berry would come into our working area every day, and sit with the troops for a long time. I always danced in my seat, at my desk, to pass the time away. Remember, employees, the military and civilians were told not to talk to Alexis, when I returned, from administrative leave. I was isolated, and my desk was facing a corner wall, so I had to entertain myself. I heard Master Sergeant Berry talking about me with MSgt Kokum, but wasn't able to hear what they were saying. "All I picked up was you haven't seen anything yet?". "Something about dancing in my seat maybe". One day I was in the break room with Cindy, and MSgt Berry went by the vending machine halfway. He turned around and came back and stopped, in the break room. I said, are you checking up on me? MSgt Berry said, yes. I said, I am right here. "I am not sure what role he plays, or is assigned to". He left, went back to his area. It was not necessary for him to go to my area. If I said anything, Cindy will fill him in later. When I talk to you, I still know everything that is going on behind me, even when a person enters the back door. Sometimes I feel things, even if not in the building. Sometimes, it's not a good feeling. It is the spirit of the Lord, when it's a need to know.

CRUELLA DEVIL

Cruella Devil was the person I told Sharon if Cruella Devil is involved, she is not a good spirit. I told Sharon that I felt nauseous in my stomach just thinking about Cruella Devil. Weeks later, Cruella Devil came downstairs to assist Mr. Mudd in placing me on a **"Performance Improvement Plan" (PIP).** I went off, on both Mr. Mudd and Cruella Devil, and pointed my finger toward them, telling them, "my performance is not questionable". I told them, "I came here to work, and this is how you treat me?". They looked at me with a "stony cold heart" and no empathy for this African American girl. I went to the travel department, told a colleague what they had done to me, and went home. I called in sick for two days. I knew that on the third day, I needed a doctor's note.

God always places me in the right place at the right time

On two occasions, I caught Cindy at Sharon's desk, and when Cindy saw me coming, she walked away from Sharon's desk. I had already seen them talking. "I see people before they see me". Sharon pretended, she and Cindy no longer had a friendship. Sharon always comes downstairs," with that Cindy drama". I act as if I didn't see them at the desk talking. I have to pretend. One day, I went out in the back rear, where the vending machine is, to use my cell phone. I saw Sharon coming out the other door dumping her trash. She saw me and came over to the double doors to get back in. Cindy came down the steps looking for Sharon, "they both busted". Sharon, with a smile, said to Cindy, "I told you I was going to meet you over there". Cindy smiled, and said okay, and walked away. I remember being tired of this behavior, "Junior high stuff", she was interfering with me, I was trying to stay positive. "They make you wanna throw up". These people act like they're "getting on-the-spot cash awards for keeping up with me", and God knows they are failing.

Warning

Before I arrived at Economical Warfare Fighter Training (EWFT), a spiritual guidance told me to watch out for two individuals. One of them was Asian or mixed, was in the military, and now a civilian. The other person has dark skin and was never in the military. . I prayed and meditated. "It was surreal."

Tamar

I was invited to Tamar's house for Christmas, and she asked me lots of personal questions. I remember returning to work while she was still on leave. I went to the budget department, where they were standing and sitting around. I said to them, it was nice of Tamar to invite me over for Christmas dinner. If you want to know something about a person, "through their name out, there and wait for a reaction". Watch their body language and facial expressions. (red flag) I noticed Lt Col Roy looked down at the floor, and no one smiled or said anything. Tamar started coming to my desk as if she were my best friend. She pretends to be a nice person, but she is not, "very quickly, she became negative". It wasn't long before she started talking about everyone in the building. It's disgusting and depressing. I like to stay in a positive spirit. My supervisor, Mr. Carter, at the time, kept getting angry with me, and I didn't know why. Then one day, he calls me into his office to go over my performance appraisal. Afterward, "he said, everybody is not your friend". I shared with Tamar how Mr. Carter treated me. "I was only venting to her, sometimes the truth hurts". I continued to talk to Tamar about life in general and stopped sharing a conversation about Mr. Carter. She didn't spear his family either. "She is a horrible person". In a twisted way, I like Mr. Carter. Tamar talked about her colleague, with whom she hangs out. I asked Tamar, don't you both do things together? She said yes, but she's not my best friend. I said okay, that's fine. Tamar was always saying things about people. I find myself always defending people, I didn't even know. Once it got so bad, she kept talking about people, until we got into an argument. She left my desk and said, "She wasn't coming back." MSgt James said, okay, goodbye. A week later, she was back at my desk. MSgt James said, "I thought you said you weren't coming back?" I thought that was funny. She told him to shut up. "That's how they roll". They were friends, but she didn't spare him, or his family. I didn't want to hear it anymore. I would talk "about apples", and she would randomly start talking about someone. Some people need to fit-in and that's Tamar. "I was exhausted". She simply cannot stay positive.

One day, I had a conversation with Faith. I wanted to warn her not to share what we talked about with Tamar, because she will tell Director Connie. I thought I was sending the text to Faith, but Tamar was in my mind and sent the text to her. Later in the week, Tamar decides to confront me. We took the conversation into the break room and Faith, to whom the text should have gone, stood there smiling. Faith said, Alexis, I thought you talked to her about this?. "Instigator" Tamar got mad and left. Part of me was sorry, but the other wasn't so sorry. Tamar has been telling Director Connie things about me. She invited me to a Country Club Ball and arranged to move to another table with her friend from out of town. She told me later that day at the Country Club Ball she moved to another table, but was not able to accommodate me. She told me, "after the fact". She said they didn't have any more seats. But she knew this going in, "set-me-up". I didn't know, that LtCol Roy would be sitting at the same table. I just met him. When I asked Tamar why she moved? She said she didn't want to hear LtCol Roy's wife, Diana, boring conversation about their kids. When I told her what LtCol Roy's wife, Diana, told me to "kiss her backside" in front of the people at the Country Club Ball. This happened when the light was on and we were seated at the front door. Tamar said you should have hugged her, and said she would have done that. The next thing that came out of my mount was "slavery is over". Do you know what she did? She walked over to Diana's table and hugged her. (red flag). Tamar told me Mr. Carter would be leaving, I said why? MSgt Kokum had an inappropriate relationship with several husbands and their wives, placed their names on the internet, and it was a big scandal. It was investigated, and that's why she left, and now she's back. Tamar said Mr. Carter said he didn't do it. I said, no way, Faith, "nod her head yes" I said, well "shut the front door". Tamar said MSgt Kokum interfered with her boyfriend, and that delayed her marriage to him. I asked Faith about that? She said no, that's not true.

Before MSgt Kokum came on board, Mr. Carter left, before she got there, like Tamar said. I couldn't dislike Mr. Carter, he is a man of God, he lost his way. 'If they got dirt on you", you will have to roll with the punches. The last thing Tamar did to me was summer of 2019. I went to the break room to relax, and Tamar followed me there. I sat in the chair, and she lay on the couch. I played with my phone as she slowly asked me questions. Then Mr. Carter came past the break room, through another area of the department. I said "out loud", I was excited to see him," Mr. Carter, and he said Hello," as he passed. Mr. Carter came back to the break room and started talking to me. Tamar got up, and told Mr. Carter, "don't talk to her, remember what she said about you?" Then she took him by his arm and said, "Come on, let's go". She was referring to what I said in the Equal Employment Opportunity complaint. Mr. Carter accused me of being late and had no proof. "I email myself every morning for three years". Remember the spiritual guidance told me to beware, watch out for two individuals? "Tamar, just exposed herself". This is what God does for "Me." "Hatred is Horrific"

FAITH

When I met Faith for the first time, she was with Tamar and Ann to welcome me to Economical Warfare Fighter Training (EWFT). Faith and Mr. Carter were the ones who invited me to Bible studies in the conference room. Faith asked me if I had a church home, and invited me to her church. Faith carried herself as if she were a sweet, nice young woman. As her friendship blossoms, she reveals her true identity. The next thing she asked me was very personal. I was uncomfortable with the questions she asked. Then she offered her husband help. She said her husband could be a good mentor to my son, and the conversation between her husband and my son will be kept private. One day, she had a yard sale. I went over to see what goodie she had. I bought a few items. One of the items was a table and chair set, she said you can make payment arrangements. I said, okay. I was going to tell her the second payment would be late. I was already struggling to pay my bills, but I needed a table because my household items were in another state. The next day after payday, Faith came to my desk. The table set was about $150-$200, not sure. She came to my "desk like a tax collector" and was aggressive. She said, "Where is my money, Alexis?" Just like that. I told her I was coming to tell you that I was going to be late. She got a little loud and said, "That is no excuse". It wasn't long before, she "showed her true color". I said I am leaving, let's walk out together. When we got outside, it got worse. She was rambling on saying it's business. "I was thinking in my mind, who is this person". The next thing that came out of her mouth was. It's not me wanting the money, it's my husband. OMG, "I hurried up and gave her the money". From time to time, when 59 minutes were given to my colleagues, I was left behind. I would see her leaving from the rear door, acting like she doesn't see me. She wouldn't even say goodnight. She tried not to look to the left when she left. I was the only one in the room with a light over my desk. I wouldn't have "cared," but every time I looked around she asked me to go to lunch with her. She would come to my desk, ask me to lunch, and even volunteer to pay for my lunch. I would say, "no thank you". I went to her house once to attend her daughter's party graduation. I never told her I see her when she leaves, she could have said later. I'm just polite. I don't think she is trustworthy. I felt empathy for her when Director Connie tried to humiliate her. One day, during the early stage of the pandemic, when masks were required. I saw her in the grocery store, but at first, I didn't recognize her. She spoke to me. I said, "Hello". She followed me to the aisle. She asked me why I stopped talking to her? I told her I didn't. I told her that I move on. "She got a little aggressive". She said, women to women, "You will tell me why you stopped talking to me?" I told her again, that I moved on. She followed me to the checkout and embarrassed me. I was so embarrassed that I lowered my head, and said nothing. Everybody stopped and looked. Some clerks stopped ringing people's orders to see if she was going to fight me. "I believe that was in their mind". That's how intense it was. She said it again. Women to women, "You will tell me why you stopped talking to me?" I said, to Faith, are you going to embarrass me, in front of all these people? I said I am sorry, I moved on. Then she walked away, saying, "I am going to pray for you". I said, thank you. Once again, God exposes her weakness.

"Maya Angelou said when people show you who they are, believe them".

Retirement Process

The Human Resources (HR) representative called me and told me she would be processing my SF52. She said I will receive my annual leave on the next payday, and see it on my leave and earnings statement on Wednesday. The HR representative said she would call me on Friday to discuss my retirement package. When HR called me on Friday, she told me she had an emergency and will call me back. She never did, and it went downhill from there. I spoke to her supervisor a week later. She was rude and thought she was just talking to anyone about the HR, Accounting Lorton, and Firm (ALAF) process. Her supervisor said the SF52 was processed last week, but she does not know how long it takes (ALAF) to process it. "What hat did she pull that out of?" It does not take two weeks for the system to generate an SF50 in the Accounts Process Pay System (APPS). I worked on both sides, Human Resource and Accounting Lorton and Firm (ALAF). I was never brief on my retirement. Finally, I received my retirement package at the end of June 2020. It took them three years of ongoing stress to cause me to have a heart attack. During the three years, I was going home crying, because I was so angry and humiliated as an African American.

I continue to pray.

Life can bring us some bad situations, but we don't have to remain bitter. We can remove bitterness from our lives by honestly repressing our feelings to God & forgiving those who have wronged us & being content with what we have. Gen 33:1-11

After the heart attack, things became more, clearly

Life is about timing, and timing is about faith, and faith is about everything. God did not promise us a perfect life. When I first arrived at Economical Warfare Fighter Training (EWFT). I ask God if this is my last assignment? He said, yes. In May 2019, I was talking to a friend about retiring. Then, in August 2019, I saw a figure of me sitting in front of me, and the spirit said retire. In December 2019, I had a heart attack. A year ago, my mother came to me in a dream. In the dream, I was in a coma. As my mother stood over me in the dream and said, "She's not dead yet." Then the dream shifts, to a few towels I sent her. The dream was confusing at the time, I didn't understand the dream. That Thursday night, when I was sitting in the hospital bed, I reflected on this dream and said it was me. I cried. I went through a storm, as my mother protected me. On December 31, 2019, I retired from (EWFT).

MAYOR RILEY PALMER REASON FOR NOT PAYING AN EMPLOYEE

Michael worked for Mayor Riley Palmer of the Forest-Townhome, doing odd jobs in the town. He completed a week of work and received his first paycheck. Mayor Palmer asked Michael to post his time for each week. Michael didn't report his time, he worked promptly. Michael continued to work for two months, without reporting his hours. Although, he kept his hour recorded on a sheet of paper. Sometimes, I would show up at Michael's location to check on him, when it gets dark. I would tell him, that's enough, come home. Michael sometimes came home muddy, and I would say, don't come in here, with that mud. Michael took 300 pictures of the work he completed and kept a spreadsheet, of the time he clocked in and out every day. Michael identified the location, and length of time he spent on each item.

Michael continued to work for two months, without reporting his hours. Although, he kept a recorded his hour on a sheet of paper. When Michael submitted his time to Major Palmer, he told Michael he would not pay him the money. Mayor Palmer said he sent people out to see if Michael was working at the location. They said Michael was not there. "How convenient" I know Michael said on many occasions, Mayor Palmer would show up at the location to check on him, and correct what he was doing wrong. Occasionally, Michael would say, Mayor Palmer, showed up at the scene to check on him, and correct what he did wrong. Michael expressed to me when he "ran out of supplies", Mayor Palmer would say he would get it for him to complete the job. One day, Mayor Palmer asked me if Michael was saved. After waiting for Mayor Palmer, he asked Captain Miller to use his credit card to buy the supply. He told Captain Miller that Mayor Palmer, secretary Kimberly, would reimburse him. When Michael took the receipt to the office, Kimberly gave him a check to reimburse, Captain. Miller. Michael bought equipment with his money, because the one Mayor Palmer gave him was inoperable. He was never reimbursed for that equipment. Mayor Palmer refused to pay him for all the work he had done. Mayor Palmer sent Michael a letter saying, "This is all he was going to pay him, and once he signed and accepted it, that would be the end of the contract." I believe it was eight months before Michael accepted the check. "God said vengeance is mine". This too shall pass.

MAYOR PALMER ERRATIC BEHAVIOR IN PUBLIC RESTAURANT

One day, I went to lunch and entered a restaurant at a place where you serve yourself buffet style, in Forest-Townhome. Mayor Palmer was there at the drinking machine. I waved to him and decided to talk to him. I express my concern about him and Michael's, not reaching an agreement. I told Mayor Palmer, I hope you guys can work it out. Mayor Palmer said, Michael took advantage of him. Mayor Palmer became aggressive. Mayor Palmer talked about how he sent people to Michael's location,

and he was never there. I kept looking at the customers, and they looked at me. **People kept looking and listening as he got louder.** "What an idiot". I walked away and returned to the salad bar. Mayor Palmer "yelled out loud that Michael better watch out, that he doesn't come up with some illegal charges". This sounds like "entrapment and corruption". That pissed me off, and **I snapped**. I walked up to him with my finger and thumb, pointed at his chest without touching him, and said: "There will not be any illegal stuff." I have already prayed about it. Then I walked back to the salad bar, and Mayor Palmer said, "I am not finished talking to you". I said to him, without looking at him, we're done! "Why did he think he can talk to this African American girl like that?" Mayor Palmer needs to look up the "definition of a role model", the title Mayor. He went back into the town, and told people that I got in his face. "I told you, I snapped". Michael came home and asked what happened between you and Mayor Palmer. "Go figure that"

PASSING BY MAYOR PALMER HOUSE

I had to pass Mayor Palmer's house to get to the parking lot of my apartment. When Mayor Palmer sees me coming, he puts his head down. One day, the Mayor was sitting on his pouch, and someone was at his fence on their bicycle. Once I passed his house, turning into my parking lot, which is directly in front of his house. I looked back in my rear-view mirror and saw Mayor Palmer pointing at me, telling this guy on the bicycle something about me. The guy looked and turned around to look at me, as I turned into my parking spot. I believe Forest-Townhome needs new leadership. New leadership could generate more revenue for Forest-Townhome. "The town needs a makeover". The people in the Forest-Town would welcome changes, they should vote him out. **"Hatred is Horrific"**

ON A DIFFERENT NOTE

One day, I was in my parking spot looking in my truck. **when a whisper said, "Look to your right"**. I looked to my right, and a man was standing on his porch, taking a picture of me. He saw me looking at him, taking my picture. He jumped back into his house. But I can see his blue shirt hanging out the door. He looked out quickly again, to see if I was still looking at him. He pokes his head out, and quickly back in. I can still see his blue shirt hanging in the door. A female was standing in the yard, watching. Finally, she told him to come on, he walked out without looking back. He walked, with her to the front, to put the trash out. "He looks ridiculous". They moved into that house a week before, he took my picture. A white cloth was hanging on the back of their house, then a man came, and took a picture. A few days later, the cloth was removed.

FALSELY CHARGE FOR A CRIME HE DID NOT COMMIT

In October 2019, Michael was retained at the front gate of Quantico for **attempting to bring CBD on board the base**. He was unaware that it was illegal on base. He never got through the gate. **Perhaps he was watched out in town** when he purchased the CBD, to alert the base he's coming through. That night, I received a call from the military police, informing me that he arrested Michael for bringing CBD through the front gate. He also informed me that if I didn't come and pick up Michael's car, it would be towed. When I arrived at the front gate, I was approached by Officer John, who was the field supervisor of the police base officer (PBO). He explained to me what happened and why Michael was arrested. Officer John said they took him to be booked, and it takes about two hours before he's released. Days later, we received a letter in the mail from the command of his charges. He was charged with three counts. One of the charges, they still tried to figure out, so they dropped it. The second charge was for trespassing on the military base. We live in Forest Townhome, "you have to come through the front gate to get to the town". The third charge was "he was falsely accused" of bringing marijuana through the front gate. **He had a receipt, he never got a chance to enjoy it.** Like I said, when I arrived, the field officer, John, the supervisor, came over to my car and said Michael brought CBD at the front gate. Officer, John, said "he unlawfully entered federal property with "CBD". While Michael was detained, the PBO who booked him said the government has not tested the THC, so they don't know how much or if marijuana is in TCH. A week later, we received the same charges from the Canyon County Prince William, Courthouse in town. The letter he received from the command stated, he could write a letter on his behalf, and appear in court, but it is not required. We submitted a letter explaining the false allegation, with a picture of Michael, in his ROTC uniform. I sent the same letter to Canyon County Prince William courthouse, and address to them. I called both the Command on Base and Canyon County Prince William courthouse. They both denied receiving the letter. I called the Canyon County Prince William courthouse clerk, and asked her if they received Michael's letter? The clerk said the letter wouldn't help him. "Go figure" That "heifer" didn't even ask me what the letter was about, she already knew who I was. The letter said Michael did not bring marijuana onboard the base, and we live in Forest-Townhome. Command on Base, said his driving privilege aboard installation has been restricted. He is only allowed to go, and come through the front gate to Forest-Townhome.

THE PROSECUTOR

In January 2020, Michael appeared in front of the Judge in Canyon County, Prince William courthouse. He was charged with bringing marijuana on federal property. The prosecutor called his first defendant. **A white male was charged for bringing CBD** through the front gate on federal property. "I believe he was a friend of the prosecutor". Let's just agree, his story sounds like Michael, an African American male". **The prosecutor asked the judge to dismiss his case,** saying the charges were CBD. "The **Judge said yes**, no problem". After the Judge said yes, the prosecutor "looked back at me, with a smirk on his face". Then the prosecutor started calling the defendants for marijuana charges. Michael was the first name, he called. The Judge asked Michael if he understood what he was being charged for? Michael said, yes. The Judge said these charges can go up to a year in prison, and a fine of five thousand dollars. "The truth of the matter" Two weeks before, appearing in court, he "total lost his car". Michael was enrolled in Purdue University, earning his second degree in Paralegal a year later, and transferred to Harvard Law School. The Judge asked Michael if he had a lawyer? He said, no. Michael told the Judge he had the money for the lawyer, but when he received the letter in the mail, he thought the whole case was dismissed. He spent the money, paying bills. The judge scheduled a later date, until Michael can retain a lawyer. He was told to "give a urine sample", it came back negative. Three days later, I called the prosecutor and told him Michael is being falsely charged. He did not have marijuana, it was CBD that he brought through the front gate. "This prosecutor didn't care". Abuse of authority. I ask the prosecutor why he dropped the charges against the "white defendant" who came through the front door with CBD? He said he had not dropped the charges on anyone. He kept repeating it over and over, that he did drop the charges on the first defendant until he said something like this. "I may have, but not the first time". I said, what do you mean? I told him I'm not going to let this go, we hung up. "Racist" "What the hell that means," but I let him know that he is charging Michael with false charges. I let him know, he is placed on "notice" that I was not going to let him get away with this". **Hatred is Horrific**

THE NEXT PHONE CALL CAME FROM THE PROBATION OFFICER

The probation officer called my cell phone, and said he was looking for Michael to schedule to meet with him. I told the probation officer, Michael, is falsely charged with the wrong crime. He had CBD that he brought through the front gate, not marijuana. I told the probation officer that Michael attended school and it became stressful, so he dis-enrolled from school. Then he asked me if we lived at "53 Boston Street, Woodcut, VA"? I said, yes. He repeated himself, asking the same question. I said we have to come through the "gate" to get to Forest-Townhome. I ask him why Michael is being charged for a crime he did not commit? He said I was not involved with that. I said, yes you are, you and the prosecutor and the judge are working together. The probation officer said, "Tell Michael to call him".

THE PROBATION OFFICER SHOWING-UP AT THE HOUSE

Michael called me and said the probation office was on his way to the house. I said, okay. I pulled up behind the probation officer, who was sitting in his car on the street. I sat there and then decided to get my mail, where he was parked, in front of the mailbox. I went back to my car, until he started going to the apartment. Then I called Michael and said, "He's on his way up the stairs". I waited and then entered the apartment and introduced myself to the probation officer. He was walking back, from the bathroom, with Michael. He stood in the kitchen, explaining to Michael that he has a chance to get probation, because this is his first offense. Michael said, "I'm not trying to get probation." He tried to convince Jack to get a public defender. Michael said, "I want to get my own lawyer". Do you remember what the Forest-Townhome, Mayor Palmer, said? He said to me in the restaurant, "Michael, better be careful that he doesn't get caught up on illegal charges?" He put his foot in his mouth. "Corrupted" Abusive of authority. Falsely accusing and framing another African American male. He told Michael to go with a public defender. Michael said he doesn't trust a public defender. The probation officer reaches in his pocket to hand Michael a card of a friend who is a public defender. I went along playing the game to see how far this probation officer would bend the rules of the law. Michael even had a receipt of the CBD he purchased. Later, the case was dropped. Why? This was an elaborate scheme to yet frame another African American male for a crime he did not commit. It's called "Racism".

JESUS BATTLED THE BULLYING AND WON!

Jesus came to bring salvation to His own, but His own rejected Him. They stripped Him, robbed Him in scarlet, stuck a crown of thorns onto His head, knelt before Him, and mocked Him. They spit on Him. They beat Him with a reed. This is the same reed they had given Him moments before to make fun of Him with a reed they stuck in His right hand as if it were a scepter. When I examine the Scripture about the crucifixion, I keep getting stuck on the word "reed," and what they did with it. It says, "They spit on Him, and took the reed and began to beat Him on the head." (Matthew 27:30) They beat Jesus with a reed. Jesus was born circa 6 B.C. in Bethlehem on Christmas day. Mary & Joseph were the parents of Jesus Christ. One day, the spirit of the Lord came to Mary and said behold. The holy spirit will come upon you, and the power will overshadow you. The child is born, and he will be called Jesus. This will be the kingdom, and he wants not to be hated. Mary asks, "How can I bear a child?" Nothing is impossible with God. God has shown you your favorite. The son, of the highest, was born on the throne of ascension David.

IN REMEMBRANCE OF MARY GARVEY LASALLE

Mrs. Mary Garvey LaSalle, who was 91 years old, a native of Atlanta, GA, died Sunday, January 2, 2011. Ms. LaSalle graduated from Girls High, worked as a commercial artist, and worked at Bell Bomber during World War II. She was married to the late Colonel Harry S. LaSalle, USAF, and they lived all over the U.S. before retiring to Beaufort, South Carolina. In 1983, Mrs. LaSalle moved to Tucker, GA, after her husband's death, to be near her family. She was a talented, artist and avid golfer, who will be remembered for her laughter and quick wit. Mrs. LaSalle reside in Beaufort National Cemetery, Beaufort, SC. I remember my first day meeting Mr. and Mrs. LaSalle. My mother took me to work, where she was a housekeeper, for the LaSalle's. They were the most down-to-earth people you would like to be around.

They give you the feeling that you are part of the family. I remember the day, Ms. LaSalle asked me if I would be interested in sitting and letting her paint my picture. I was so excited that she wanted to paint me. I came with my mother on many occasions and went to various locations to sit and have my picture painted. I remember having my picture painted on the beach and sitting in the window seal. Then she would attend an art exhibit to sell her painting. One day, Mrs. LaSalle said Alexis, would you like one of your paintings? I said yes. I still have the painting today, to remember Mrs. LaSalle enjoyed painting me. Thank you, Mr. and Mrs. LaSalle, for being part of my life. Memories of you have been a blessing to me and others, which you embrace even after you have gone to heaven.

MEMORIES OF EVERLENA AND MARY

She was a person who thought about others, before thinking about herself. Her sister-in-law encouraged her to move her family to Beaufort, South Carolina. Through her faith and compassion for the needy, she decided to beat the odds, and do something positive, within the community. Every summer, she began renting a room in her home to seasonal workers. She fed many of the military members stationed at the Air Base, Beaufort, and the Recruit Depot, Parris Island. She allowed those serving in the military to find a home away from home, and they called her "Sugar Mama".

She was a gift to those in her surroundings and others. Everlena had "an awesomely, incredibly close friend" named Mary Linnen, they were like sisters. They were the best of friends. "They both were intuitive people". On Sundays, they loved going to each other's church to fellowship. Every night, Everlena and Mary called each other, and talked on the phone for hours, until one of them fell asleep. After my mother went home to "our Heavenly Father". Before returning to California, Ms. Mary called me and started talking for hours, as she did my mother. Ms. Mary had some interesting conversation, we talked for hours. God gave me patience, she missed her best friend. My brother walked past me and said, "who are you talking to?" Ms. Mary. He said, "Oh," you're now Ms. Mary's girlfriend, since Mama is gone, and smiled.

Every time I think of these ladies, I smile. "Incredible humble"

In memory of Anderson Williams, who died on May 28, 1997
In memory of Jessie-Rae Williams Whitehead Christian, who died on May 30, 2013
In memory of Anthony Williams, who died on March 17, 2017.

May Everlena and Mary, memories, be a blessing to those who embrace them while they were here. For the beautiful and loving souls inside of them. Rest in peace.

ACKNOWLEDGMENT, THANK YOU

- To my brother James, thank you for taking care of me since I was a little girl. If I had any concerns, I would wait until you come home on military leave to tell you my problems. When I told James that I was moving to California, he came to Atlanta, GA, and packed my household items in a U-Haul, and then took them to Beaufort, S.C., which allowed me to move on to California.

After the passing of my mother, Cynthia said she would be my son, Michael'sGodmother. Cynthia, thank you for being there for my son, Michael, and me mentally and physically, when we needed you. I had always told her that Michael is her son. He truly loves her and calls her for support. He had always felt that she gives good advice. Cynthia has an amazing best friend name, Lafrance. She has always been a big sister to me growing up. When my mother spank my butt, I would run across the street to her house and cry to her. She would explain to me why I got my butt spank and send me on my way. She calls it tough love. Cynthia and Lafrance have been best friends since they were little kids growing up. When Cynthia and Lafrance smile, you see their beautiful soul and spirit inside of them. They are beautiful and loving Christians. I would like to salute James, and Cynthia, for their support of me coming up. Thank you, I love you.

- I would like to thank a colleague, Mrs. S. A., for her support for me during my time at Economical Warfare Fighter Training (EWFT), notice the 59 minutes. She was the only one who spoke out about what she saw. "Fairless" The late John Lewis says if you see something, say something. Thank you, Mrs. S.A.

- I would like to thank Mr. D. H. from Economical Warfare Fighter Training (EWFT). I met a nice young man, whom I admire. I did not know him personally, I always greet him in the morning coming in to work. He would either get out of his car or pull up in the parking lot. He always had time to say nice, pleasant words. He had a kind spirit that shined inside and outside his heart. When I mentioned to him that I was leaving, and I had a heart attack, I got very emotional. He told me to let it go, and that it will be alright. He reached out his hands to me, and started praying for me. That was one of the kindest things in my three years at (EWFT), that anyone ever showed empathy for what I was going through. He is truly a child of God. Thank you, Mr. D. H.

- I would like to thank a young lady I met in 2004. I worked for Accounting Lorton and Firm (ALAF), and she needed my assistance in resolving pay problems. Throughout the years, we stayed in contact, even when I transferred to Accounting Lorton and Firm (ALAF) in Indianapolis, Indiana. When Accounting Lorton and Firm (ALAF) Cleveland had their Customer Service Representative Conference, we got the chance to meet each other face-to-face. She has been a tremendous friend in a time of need. When I felt my lowest, I can call her day or night and cry on her shoulders. One day, I learned, Oprah, if you're reading this, "she has a picture of her and Mr. Stedman Graham". I said to her, "What are you doing in a picture with Oprah man?" She started laughing at me and said he was a guest speaker at the Administrative and Secretary Conference. Thank you, Ms. R.T. Everything, check out Oprah and Mr. Stedman.

- I would like to thank Mr. S.M. for being a real trooper. I remembered when he received his promotions, he always threw a party. His party starts at 11:30 a.m. until the next day at 11:30 a.m. I don't know how he does it. He started cooking the night before the party. He knew how to cook everything. If you name it, he will cook it in Louisiana style. He asks you to bring your own bottles. He invites any and everybody, even the colleagues at Accounting Lorton and Firm (ALAF). It was always the word of the mount, and almost everyone from (ALAF) shows up. I went for lunch and then returned, after work. Did I tell you he cooks so much food? He insisted you take food home. He is an awesome cook and entertainer. He plays oldies records from way back in the days. If you named a song, he had it. When my son and I were leaving Indianapolis, Indiana, he threw a party for us. I would like to thank Mr. S.M. for the kindness, generosity, and hospitality he shared with his colleagues and others. For that, I salute you, Mr. S.M US Army. I love you

- I would like to thank my son, Michael, for being part of my life. We may not always "see eye to eye", but I know you love your mother. The gift connects us with God, who has given us "His grace and mercy". I always tell you to have faith, to remain in the word, trust only, our Lord Savior. Lord, I thank you for allowing me to share your spiritual, child with you. Thank you Michael, I love you from the bottom of my heart.

- I would like to thank Pastor E.S.W., for calling me wherever I was in the world, you called. As I went through something, God heard my cry, he sent you Pastor E.W. "You said, Alexis, I have a word for you from God", which brought tears to my eyes. I was wounded, I needed it at that moment. Thank you for your continuous support. I love you.

- Thank you, Mrs. A. S-M. When I was in the hospital, you immediately came and protected me when I had a heart attack. When they placed me in an induced coma, the spirit led you to feel my body, and it was cold. It was you, alerted the doctor. The doctor then positioned me, so my body can return to normal. Thank you so much, Mrs. A.S, for being my protector. Thank you, Ms. D.W-D. God told you to call Mrs. A.S. to stand by my hospital bed. "It's the same dream I had". Through Christ Jesus, my Lord and Savior, you save my life. I love you, sisters.

- I would like to thank the Equal Employment Opportunity Counselor in Virginia for their knowledge, skills, and support within their EEO policies.

- I would like to thank you, Heavenly Father, for choosing me, Alexis, to go on this long journey, to be there for those who have been unethical mistreated. I always felt your Holy Spirit upon me and protected me. I trust you, and only you, Father God, 100% Faith.

SOME OF FEW SONGS TO REFLECT "LOVE AND CHANGE"

These are some of the song's, I can relate to when I have that moment, and also make

- **Michael Jackson**-Man in the Mirror I'm starting with the man in the mirror, asking him to change his way. If you wanna make the world a better place, take a look at yourself and then make a change. "called for

- **Kirk Franklin**- He Loves Me. He loves me even when I fall beneath His will. He loves me. Even though He knew sometimes I'd fall, yet still my name He called He loves me. "When

- **Beyoncé**, if I were a Boy, I think I could understand. How it feels to love a girl. I swear I'd be a better man. I'd listen to Her "Cause I know How It Hurts. "When I was dating, I thought like a man to please him without losing myself".

- **Billie Eilish**- Your Power. Try not to abuse your power I know we didn't choose to change. You might not wanna lose your power But haven' it's so strange. "Love the lyrics. I listen to many of

- **Alicia Keys and Jay-Z**- New York, New York. Concrete jungle (yeah) where dreams are made of There's nothin' you can't do (Yeah) (Okay) Now you're in New York. "It brings "chill down my spin

- **Christopher Cross** - Sailing. Well, it's not far down to paradise at least it's not for me. "Love the hook" Sailing takes me away. "Soon I will be free.

Summary

This started from an Equal Employment Opportunity Complaint I filed in 1993, on the Park-Red Base in California. I file a Sexual Harassment case against my supervisor, Mr. Freeman and won. This case was not about a monetary award. This case was about correcting my performance appraisal and harassment. I was not the only one he was inappropriate with.

The agency try to convince me there is no Discrimination in the Workplace: They close my case. I just keep appealing until I get to the Supreme Court.

"What you should know"

- The agency frowns when you file an EEO complaint
- African Americans will not move up if you file an EEO complaint.
- The agency is becoming more aggressive in its behavior and "Bold".
- If you file an EEO complaint, you must have some tongue skin.
- Once you have filed an EEO complaint, your work environment will change.
- Your colleagues will distance themselves from you because of the management.

- They will charge you with false charges.
- They will encourage the employee not to talk to you if he wants to move up.
- I was a friend of both white and black colleagues.

The white girl told me that management told her to stay away from the black girl if she wanted to move up. She caught me off guard, and I snapped. We were good friends. I don't like people telling me who I should not talk to. I apologize to her.

- You are a victim, but they treat you as if you had committed a crime.
- They sabotage your work.

- You feel trapped in a system, and know you will not move up. You ask   yourself, where can I go?
- They'll try to push you out.
- Most lawyers are blocked from taking your case. They take your case and lose it on purpose. "Threaten"
- I have seen it with friends, of mine, that I was helping with their case.
- When you leave, this EEO complaint follows you to the next agency.
- They disrespect you, humiliate you, make you feel incompetent, and their nothing you can do.
- Your Progress review will show that you are not fulfill your responsibility.
- They contact people outside your office who know you and start a train wreck. It depends on how bad they want you to get out. These are horrible people

I read about a judge who filed an EEO complaint, because he was promised a promotion. Once he filed, everything went downhill for the judge. They target his family. His story sound like, many others. Did I tell you he was an African American?

- These people are horrible. This is the life in which we live today.
- If it weren't for the Lord Jesus Christ, I wouldn't know where I would be today. 100% faith. I know him so well.
- We are working together to bring about changes. That is what he told me.
- He has been whispering in my ear for a long time in my career. I feel his presence always.
- I looked back at my life, and started crying. The mighty creator has been preparing me for this day.
- Every time someone tries to hurt me, he has my back. He said vengeance is mined.
- He has something extraordinary for those who suffer, and those who tried to help, but their hands were tired. He hears your cry.
- One day, I was sitting on the couch and I said, Lord, what is this all about? He said, Jesus. OMG I started weeping.
- I can promise you that this EEO complaint against African Americans and any Brown people will change. It can not stay like this.
- Please trust your Creator, He will carry you through.
- I have seen things happen to people who tried to wrestle with me.
- It is not me. I am just the messenger.
- I am not scared and I am not alone. 100% faith. Humble and respectfully

When the agency has "dirt on you," this is how you behave

I can't breathe

- Michelle Obama said when they go low, you go high.
- Maya Angelou said if they show you who they are, believe them.
- John Lewis said if you see something, say something.
- Oprah Winfrey said What I Know For Sure.

God's Child

I have always told people when they attack me, they attack the Holy Spirit in me. Under this skin is "God" that you are attacking. In my mind, "I say, go ahead". This is just my face, I'm just the messenger. I try not to say anything negative about people, because it's not pleasing to the Heavenly Father. He has given me so much power, and I am heavily protected by "His" namesake through Christ Jesus, my Lord and Savior. 100% faith.

Do not avenge yourselves, beloved, but leave room for God's wrath. For it is written "Vengeance is Mine" Romans 12:19 NIV

Legislation

I will fight for you to bring about change. People have the right to "demand justice" in the workplace when management mistreated them. "No one is above the law". I will work on passing a bill for people affected by the "Whistleblower" and Equal Employment Opportunity, complaint against management. This Bill will allow you to get counseling for PTSD, among other things will happen. "Time is on my side.

Title VII of the Civil Rights Act of 1964: Makes it illegal to discriminate against someone on the basis of race, color, religion, national origin or sex. This law also protects employees against retaliation for going forward with a claim regarding discrimination in the workplace

Printed in the United States
by Baker & Taylor Publisher Services